The Multiversity

The

Nicholas von Hoffman

Multiversity

A Personal Report on

What Happens to Today's Students

at American Universities

Holt, Rinehart and Winston

New York   Chicago   San Francisco

Published simultaneously in Canada by Holt, Rinehart
and Winston of Canada, Limited.

Library of Congress Catalog Card Number: 66-14222

First Edition

Designer: Ernst Reichl
89078-0116
Printed in the United States of America

Acknowledgments

Grateful acknowledgment is made to the following for their permission to include selections from the books and periodicals listed:

The Trustees of Amherst College for an excerpt from "What the Liberal College Is" by Alexander Meiklejohn in *The Liberal College* (1920).

Appleton-Century-Crofts for an excerpt from *Life and Confessions of a Psychologist* by G. Stanley Hall (1923).

Basic Books, Inc., Publishers, New York, for an excerpt from *The Academic Marketplace* by Theodore Caplow and Reece J. McGee (1958).

Columbia University Press, New York, for an excerpt from *The Old-Time College President* by George P. Schmidt (1930).

Crown Publishers, Inc., for excerpts from *Revolt on Campus*, copyright 1935 by James Wechsler (1935).

Harper & Row, Publishers, Inc., for an excerpt from *Changing Values in College: An Exploratory Study of the Impact of College Teaching* by Philip E. Jacob (1957).

Harvard University Press for an excerpt from "Academic Freedom" by Abbott Lawrence Lowell in *At War With Academic Traditions in America* (1934); and for an excerpt from "Non Economic Aspects of Academic Morals" by Everett C. Hughes, edited by Seymour E. Harris, in *Higher Education in the United States*.

Harvard University Press and The Belknap Press for an excerpt from *Three Centuries of Harvard, 1636–1936* by Samuel Eliot Morison (1936).

Holt, Rinehart and Winston, Inc., for an excerpt from *Alma Mater* by Henry Seidel Canby (1936). Copyright © 1964 by Marion Ponsonby Gause Canby.

Human Relations Aids for excerpts from *The Revolt of the College Intellectual* by Everett Lee Hunt (1963).

Alfred A. Knopf, Inc., for an excerpt from *The American College and University: A History* by Frederick Rudolph (1962).

McGraw-Hill Book Co., Inc., for an excerpt from *Graduate Education in the United States* by Bernard Berelson (1960), and for an excerpt from *Higher Education: Resources and Finance* by Seymour E. Harris (1962).

The Nation for an excerpt from "Custodians of the Language Convene" by Wade Thompson, Vol. cc, No. 6.

Oxford University Press, Inc., for an excerpt from *The Uses of the Past: Profiles of Former Societies* by Herbert Muller (1957); for an excerpt from *Illinois* by Allan Nevins (1917); for an excerpt from *The Academic Man* by Logan Wilson (1942); and for an excerpt from *Ludwig Wittgenstein, a Memoir* by Norman Malcolm.

Princeton University Press for an excerpt from *Princeton, 1746–1896* by Thomas Jefferson Wertenbaker.

Sing Out! for an excerpt from "Songs from Berkeley" by Irwin Silber, Vol. 15, No. 2, May 1965.

University of Chicago Press for permission to reprint excerpts from the books listed below that appeared in *American Higher Education: A Documentary History*, edited by Richard Hofstadter and Wilson Smith (1961) two volumes: *Thoughts on the Present Collegiate System in the United States* by Francis Wayland (1842), Vol. I; *University Education* by Henry P. Tappan (1851), Vol. II; *Johns Hopkins University Celebration of the Twenty-fifth Anniversary of the Founding* by Daniel Cort Gilman (1902), Vol. II; *Oberlin, Its Origin, Progress, and Results. An Address . . . 1860* by J. H. Fairchild (1871), Vol. I; *Letters on College Government* by Frederick A. P. Barnard (1896); *Yale Report of 1828*, Vol. I; *Address to the Inhabitants of Jamaica, and Other West Indian Islands in Behalf of the College of New Jersey* by John Witherspoon (1772), Vol. I; *The New Departure in College Education, Being a Reply to President Eliot's Defense of It in New York* by James McCosh (1885), Vol. II; "The Trustees of Dartmouth College *v.* Woodward," in *Reports of Cases Signed and Decided in the Supreme Court of the United States,* IV (1882), Vol. I; *An Autobiography* by Julian M. Sturtevant (1896); and *The Works of Philip Lindsley,* edited by L. J. Halser (1866).

University of Nebraska Press for an excerpt from *Constraint and Variety in American Education* by David Riesman (1956).
D. Van Nostrand Co., Inc., for an excerpt from *What College Students Think* by Rose K. Goldsen and others, copyright 1960, D. Van Nostrand Company, Inc., Princeton, N.J.

The Viking Press, Inc., for excerpts from *The Higher Learning in America: A Memorandum on the Conduct of Universities by Businessmen* by Thorstein Veblen (1918).

John Wiley & Sons, Inc., for permission to reprint excerpts from the articles that appeared in *The American College,* edited by Nevitt Sanford (1962): "The Viability of the American College" by David Riesman and Christopher Jencks, "The Teacher as Model" by Joseph Adelson, "Dropouts from College" by John Summerskill, and "Changing Functions of the College Professor" by Robert H. Knapp.

Yale University Press for an excerpt from *Mark Hopkins and the Log* by Frederick Rudolph (1956); for an excerpt from *Illinois College: A Centennial History, 1829–1929* by Charles Henry Rammelkamp (1928); for an excerpt from *Yale College, 1871–1921* by George Wilson Pierson (1952); and for excerpts from *The Higher Learning in America* by Robert M. Hutchins (1936).

To Ginny and Larry Fanning

When one considers in its length and in its
breadth the importance of this question of
the education of a nation's young, the broken
lives, the defeated hopes, the national failures,
which result from the frivolous inertia with
which it is treated, it is difficult to restrain
within oneself a savage rage.

Alfred North Whitehead

Contents

ix

The Multiversity
A Personal Report

Going to college will soon be the universal American experience.
Already half of this generation's youth have had at least a taste of
it. However, colleges come in many flavors and they don't taste
alike.

The word college covers downtown night schools, girls' semi-
naries run by nuns, technical institutes, the liberal arts colleges
featuring Georgian architecture and elm trees, normal schools,
community or junior colleges, and the colleges that are part of
old private universities and the great state universities. All are
colleges, and none of them is the same in the kind or quality of
education they offer.

All confer the bachelor's degree that entitles you to a job, but
some—the universities—are more important than others. They
are the models and the molders of higher education. They train
the college teachers, they set the standards and the pace. At the
most, there are no more than eighty true universities. (Many that
use the title are colleges with a few graduate departments.) Except for the older private universities, they are indescribably big,
diffuse, and specialized. You cannot write about all of them ex-
haustively; that job would take a battalion of scholars scores of
years. Even an exact description of one—one of the small ones

xi

like Yale or Princeton—would call for the expert talent of many men writing and studying many years.

Nevertheless, these institutions must be written about because of the power they have, because of the mark they put on our most gifted young men and women, and because lately the nation has been made aware that the universities are troubled within themselves. Most of the writing about universities in the past few years —by teachers, administrators, students, and social critics—has either been polemical or has assumed a knowledge of university life —an institutional experience—that people outside it don't often have. They need to know about it, however. Universities are playing too influential a role in this society of technology and expertise to permit public ignorance about them.

This book hopes to supply a substitute for first-hand knowledge by describing what one university is like to the people who live in it. It is a book of travel to the campus, an account of a short voyage to a modern university. It is not offered as sociology or as a scholarly work; it is a form of journalism which first took shape as an article for the Chicago *Daily News,* and the minimal notes and references have been relegated to the end.

Its title was popularized by Clark Kerr, president of the University of California, and, while "multiversity" is a vogue word which will probably pass out of fashion in a few years, its use now serves to remind us that the university of today is no longer a playpen for a few upper-class children irrelevant to a society of busy workers doing the other important tasks needing to be done.

The school picked for this visit is the University of Illinois at Champaign-Urbana. One might ask whether it can be used as representative of American universities. The answer is that there is no way of demonstrating to everybody's satisfaction which university may be representative. The most that can be said, as this book tries to show, is that all the major universities have had an approximately parallel development, and that they are now organized and run in about the same way, with identical goals and values. This is not to say they are all the same, however.

Berkeley, for instance, is very different from Illinois and most of the other great universities. Berkeley presides over a fully developed system of other state university campuses and colleges. This is the direction most of the major state universities are traveling, but the other colleges and university campuses in their satellite systems are not yet so specialized or so fully matured. Berkeley and some other schools more famous than Illinois were ruled out for this study on the grounds that both their faculties and student bodies were so superior as to be nonrepresentative.

Harvard was an impossible choice, because Harvard is Harvard; there is still nothing like its influence and prestige.

The other private universities were not selected for several reasons. The first is that although they have a national eminence, they tend to dominate higher education in only one section of the country—the Northeast. Elsewhere, state universities either dominate or share the prominence. Even in the Northeast, New York and Massachusetts have had to cease relying on private schools and start spending significant sums of money on their state institutions.

A second reason for not using the private university is the possibility that its day is done. They don't have as much money as the state schools, and were it not for the federal government, private universities might already have been entirely overshadowed by their younger, publicly owned rivals. (A 1963 report by the Carnegie Foundation shows schools such as the University of Chicago, Princeton, and Stanford getting over forty percent of their budgets from Washington.) However, old grads, sad at the thought that their alma maters are irreversibly in decline, still have reason for hope. The private schools are stubbornly fighting the public ones by lobbying to make state schools raise their tuition and fees to keep private schools competitive, and by supporting loan and scholarship programs as against a system of free higher education.

Ohio State or the University of Nebraska or any of several dozen other places might have been picked as the destination of this voyage, but there were good reasons arguing for Illinois. This university is considered to be the worst of the best—that is, it is number ten on the list of the ten best universities. Not that there really is any accepted way of rating universities, but when lists are drawn, Illinois comes up looking as though it has one foot planted in greatness and the other in mediocrity.

Illinois is the nation's third largest maker of Ph.D.'s, and its faculty ranks eighth among faculties in the forced feeding of articles into academic journals. It has a Nobel Prize winner, and a library that rival librarians say is first-rate, but it also has a cow-college flavor and a number of departments in the humanities and social sciences which even its officials concede are "weak." Although the majority of students are in the liberal arts curriculum, as they are at other places, the institution has many students in vocational programs. Thus its campus is a good place to see various tugs and pulls which beset the modern university: liberal arts versus vocational training; cosmopolitan academic rigor versus the older emphasis on teaching without research; the intellectual campus culture against the comforting and settled social life represented by the Greek (fraternity) system; outside business and government work versus the older idea of scholastic separation and detached concentration.

This book, then, is an attempt to take the old bromide that education is experience and see what that experience means to the individual in the institution, be he student, administrator, or teacher. But it is extremely difficult to describe the impact of an institution with any precision, as the social scientists, who have tried, will testify. The scenes and the people in this book do not represent a cross section but were chosen because they illustrate the human dimensions of the problems agitating the modern university. The unusual, the extraordinary, are used to suggest the usual, the ordinary, the way it is day by day. But the way it is day by day in a university can be confusing if you have no idea how it got that way, and for this reason the book includes a selection of materials—necessarily incomplete—on the history of higher education in the United States. These selections should make it clear that the present generation of university administrators is more the inheritors than the inventors of practices currently under attack.

The universities' present service to war research, government and corporate enterprise is not, whatever else it may be, an abandonment of older, better, and purer policies and practices. American colleges and universities have never been cloistered and independent of society; they have never been places which nurtured dissent and social change. From their beginnings they have served immediate and publicly stated needs; the people who now look upon them as special redoubts of freedom are not restoring an old definition but making a new one. As history shows, change in an American university is not easily accomplished. One of the points made in this book is that American universities can add new studies, new activities, or new organizations with relative ease, but must torture themselves to make any change in what already exists. It is easier for them to join with three other schools to build a new multimillion-dollar research facility than to revise the freshman English requirements, or—more drastic yet—make adjustments in the institution which would alter relations between people.

This is not because university people are blind or indifferent. Perhaps the greatest irony in higher education is the way in which it breeds such a large body of articulate criticism. "The university . . . grew . . . to include its own severest critics," says Laurence R. Veysey in "The Emergence of the American University" (University of Chicago Press, 1965, p. 442), a study that shows just peradventure that, whatever their problems may be, academicians certainly haven't been oblivious of them.

Now, as in the past, there is no end of witty, well-spoken, bitterly critical students, teachers, and administrators, and they are not by any means all lower-echelon malcontents. They are just as likely to be brilliant university presidents as freshmen or unknown graduate students. Yet it seems that the more the university administration knows about what is wrong with their institution the more helpless they feel in the face of their problems. The university's capacity to change is astonishingly weak; this is one reason we see students going to such lengths to push their schools toward new ways. Nineteenth-century American college students had to set up libraries for themselves and start their own science programs because their schools would not. Twentieth-century students, with well-equipped libraries and laboratories, have different problems, but must still deal with a monumental institutional inertia.

To be changed the system must be understood. The institution resists change because its primary characteristic is the diffusion and fragmentation of the power to effect change. This fragmentation of power reaches back to the founding of Harvard. The school's small size and its youthful instructors made it unwise to follow the pattern of the English universities and place power in the hands of the senior faculty. Since there was no senior faculty except the president, a board of overseers, or trustees, was set up, and this has become the American pattern. Whatever the quality of people who comprise a lay, off-campus board, they are bound to act with great caution, if for no other reason than the fear of making a mistake in a situation with which they can have little familiarity. In fact, most university boards have shown themselves to be almost totally immobile. They are often a generation or two behind in their understanding of contemporary needs, and since their membership is customarily drawn from the rich and influential, they are the most likely to be satisfied with the way things are and the least likely to sympathize with the urgings for change.

Universities are too complicated for their trustees to understand or govern save in the most general way. A trustee has about the same grasp of what his institution is doing as an ordinary congressman has of what the Department of Defense is doing. Much of the real power to change a university, therefore, has been cut up and apportioned between the departments and the administration. The biggest departments, which bring in the most research money, have the greatest power, but departmental power is also divided among people owning various-sized shares in the academic patronage system of fellowships, research grants, and outside moneys. Hence, university committees and academic senates rarely rise above logrolling and the dividing of spoils.

For the academician in the right specialty, there are more spoils to divide than ever before. In fact, there are now professors who never teach, never research, who are only go-betweens from their departments to foundations, business, and government. They are the executives who manage our corporate academic research, and they, too, have a special power in the running of a university. The man who can bring in the business, the research money, to feed the graduate students and enhance the size and reputation of his department—and his university—will obviously have a strong voice in major decisions.

As useful as the academic entrepreneur may be to a nation that does its scientific investigations by *levée en masse* of graduate students and underprofessors, the arrangement works against change in the university itself. For any basic change in the organization of the modern university would involve a change in the position of the student in relation to his teachers and to research—that is, the serious work of the university—and that, in turn, means a change in the patterns of recruiting people into departmental specializations and in the whole complicated system of rank and awards.

Another force inhibiting a university's changing is other universities. As the system now operates, thousands of anonymous students must be anonymously interchangeable; one school must not initiate a change unacceptable to the others. This puts a premium on keeping undergraduate education as it is. Interchangeability of credits is most important for undergraduates because they are the most numerous and the most mobile; but the best undergraduates in the best universities are among the most discontented by bureaucratized schooling, which appears to them—and many of their teachers—as a continuation of all the defects of high school, along with the impersonality of the immense, modern, busybodying university.

With certain notable and noble exceptions the universities have, albeit not deliberately, pursued policies which seem bound to make their internal contradictions more painful.

On the one hand they have pressured the high schools to raise their standards (and by a number of devices the great state universities ultimately have a ruling power over high schools). The results are showing in large numbers. The better suburban high schools are now graduating incomparably well-prepared students. Unfortunately for the universities, these students are more than bookishly precocious. They are more experienced and less docile. Maturing earlier physically, they often come to the universities already partially initiated into the skeptical, doubting, and rational intellectual culture of the West. They attend the university with the same objectives as their teachers so that they find the regulations and the institutional responses, designed for the student of the past who waged war on the faculty and academic work, especially irritating and absurd.

On the other hand, the universities have reinforced practices that are bound to irk such young adults by asking of them, through the dorm system, through high-school-like curriculums, a docility they no longer have. Moreover, the universities make the problem worse by continuing to raise their admission standards. In this way they bring more of these critically minded high-school graduates onto their campuses, all the while displacing those students who are less likely to be restive. Once the new kind of student is on campus he is nudged into the liberal arts curriculum and away from the *déclassé* vocational schools.

One of the results of the new state system of higher education is to let the major state university hand over lower-class vocational education to the lesser colleges and universities in the pedagogical grid. Halbert E. Gulley, head of the Division of General Studies at the University of Illinois, says of this practice: "It ought to be possible to have in every state a high-quality university that stands for depth and excellence. One of my heresies is to go much farther than we have, to develop what I like to call diversities and opportunity. Since people think college is essential for their children—just about everybody does today—we can assign status to vocational training by calling these schools colleges, and this would leave the university free to do its work."

A gigantic campus of thousands of early maturing people, all feeding on the restlessness and questioning liberal arts tradition, must be an accommodating institution or face the possibility of serious trouble. One example of trouble materialized at Berkeley in the winter of 1964-1965, but most of the big universities have not gone quite so far in their development. They are more like Illinois, an institution in transition, moving in Berkeley's direction as a new kind of student and faculty member replaces the old in a slowly changing institution. Serious trouble for them still lies in the future.

The specific problem at Berkeley arose over what the insurgents called "free speech," that is, their right to use a few feet of university-owned cement sidewalk to solicit for civil rights demonstrations, which might or might not be illegal. Very soon after the student disturbances started, however, their invective turned against the whole university—the "machine" they called it—and then the root of the problem was exposed—that is, the claim of students, graduate and undergraduate, to some real share in the running of the university. Needless to say, this is not the same as asking for a student government, which is a masquerade, like the civic youth events when a high-school student is allowed to be mayor for a day. At Berkeley the request was for a real share of genuine power now held by the board of trustees, the president, the faculty, and such outside interests as the government and other funding agencies.

The idea may strike some people as tantamount to giving guns to children—letting students take part in the formal running of a university, hiring faculty, working on curriculums, voting on the allocation of funds—but the student who is coming to dominate universities such as Illinois enters the university with a better, broader training than many collegians of forty years ago had when they were graduated. A few smaller liberal arts colleges with this kind of select student body have already shared the governing of the institution with their students. The results have neither been academic bolshevism nor perfection.

In the past the unhappy student has been told that if he does not like it where he is, he should go elsewhere; but going from one university to another is like walking up on the down escalator—a great deal of traveling to stay in the same place. The student can leave school entirely, yet in this society only the boldest will attempt the intellectual life without credentials. So the student must stay and undergo our academic *rites de passage,* which never take less than four years, and often two or three times as long before full adulthood, in the form of a doctor's gown, is granted him. It is not a figure of speech to equate the Ph.D. with full adulthood, full citizenship. In the past it was enough to guarantee a man's civil liberties, but even with your civil liberties, if you are a student in an all-embracing institution like a modern university, you can still be in a servile condition.

In a society that depends on more and ever larger institutions, the older definitions of personal liberty are not adequate. We are going to have to invent new sets of inalienable rights for ourselves. The need to do so may soon be pressing in the major universities where the collegiate adolescent is being replaced by young adults. The visible changes at the University of Illinois make this clear, as they also make clear that changes in dormitory regulations are not going to meet students' discontent and coming demands.

I hope the following pages will explain what these demands are and show that many of them are not particularly new or radical. Indeed, a surprising number are restatements of what the best American educators have been saying for the better part of a century.

But can universities change? Or are they, as some educators say, no more than part of the "knowledge industry," which is so locked in with other industries and government that any organic change is impossible? Before surrendering to such pessimism, universities might do well to bring their graduate and undergraduate students into their government. The students—and large blocs of critical faculty members and administrators—may then be able to create in these institutions organs of power strong enough to overcome Whitehead's "frivolous inertia."

February 24, 1966   —Nicholas von Hoffman

The Multiversity

I

Success Story

From a distance across the quadrangle's geometry of sidewalks,
the crowd of perhaps thirty jumping, jerking, bending, stamping
boys seemed to be dancing to unheard music of disrupted rhythm.
Some of them, hooded against a nearly windless cold, looked like
the chief celebrants of an antic ritual as they raised arms and
gloved hands upward over their heads or pointed argumentative
fingers at closely buttoned chests.

There was still sun in the sky but the freezing air and the
light's low energy made the young men, despite the disputative
dance, monochromes. The dullness of the winter colors and the
place of the gesticulating argument, the lower gray stone steps of
the domed gold auditorium building, suggested that they were
players in a modern film who had come to do their dance by the
approaches to an old, old temple.

On the quadrangle nearly deforested by Dutch Elm Disease,
people were hurrying to lunch, laboratory, and library in the
early afternoon cold. They had no time for students who
screamed at each other.

"War! War! War! Defoliate the valleys! Murder the peasants!
Kill everybody. You're a hawk, a hawk!" "Appeasement," came
the retort. "Isolationism. We're tired of losing."

3

"Your party's the isolationist party," the first student screamed back. "You're the ones that didn't want to arm. It's always been the conservatives who're the isolationists. You were responsible for appeasing Hitler."

"And what about China, and Korea, and the Berlin Wall? What about Hungary and the Freedom Fighters?"

A half a dozen other arguments of this sort were being waged by young men with faces so white with cold that the ground of their beards and the red spots on their cheeks stood out against their pallor. The auditorium at the quadrangle's south end, a building reminiscent of the Pantheon in Rome, is the traditional place of student protest at the University of Illinois. Here, a few minutes before, about fifty people had met to object to the war in Viet Nam. Most of the objectors were members of the campus Young Democrats, and of Students for a Democratic Society (SDS), a left-wing, intellectual student grouping which, although it is national in having chapters on many of the leading campuses, is too anarchistic in its membership to be called an organization.

The protestors had been heckled by members of a right-wing student group, Young Americans for Freedom (YAF), who carried nicely lettered signs saying things like "Don't Negotiate Away the Life of 15 Million Vietnamese." At the end of the formal protest, hecklers and heckled had joined in shouting, man-to-man, verbal combats while cold drops of moisture clung to the tips of their noses. Their words were wildly accusatory and illogical; their tone was a mixture of anger and mirth. It was as though they felt they should hate each other but could not, because it was a game in which there are no prizes for the winner, no penalties for the loser. (Students so often talk about the "real world outside," where the score is really kept and the winning and the losing really count.)

John Johnson, in a black-and-white car coat, stood a step or two higher than most of the shouting young men, his hands in his pockets, a loose-leaf notebook wedged under his arm, feet apart

4

as though straddling an object that only he saw. Suddenly he bent forward and bellowed down at a blond-bearded student in a blue parka:

"Yeah? What about the satellite countries? What about Poland, Hungary, Rumania and Yugoslavia?"

"Yeah?" The blue parka shouted back up to John. "What do you know about Yugoslavia?"

"There's no freedom there. Religion is suppressed. The people would revolt if they could."

"Which shows you, you don't know anything about Yugoslavia. Where'd you get your information? Where?" the blue parka wanted to know.

"I talked to a Roman Catholic priest, a Yugoslavian who escaped," John said, then added in soft astonishment to himself as much as to the blue parka, "and I'm not a Catholic."

"Well, it so happens," the blue parka exclaimed, "I've spent six months in Yugoslavia. Why don't you ask me? My wife is still there. She's spent eleven months there working on her thesis. We know what the situation is."

Bested by on-the-spot knowledge, John turned away to find someone else to argue with. As I listened to him, it was hard to tell whether he was serious about what he was saying. He seemed a competitive personality. Just twenty-one years old, he would be slight of build if he did not exercise regularly. Too small for varsity athletics, he had participated in intramural sports during his four and a half years at the University of Illinois.

My hands and feet were beginning to get cold, so I shouted, "Let's have lunch. I'll buy." He argued for a few more minutes, and then we walked, our breath vaporizing in the freezing air, to the expensive restaurant in the brick, Georgian Illini Union building. On the way John offered an explanation for the shouting contest. "We're the fascists and they're the communists."

He did not mean it literally, but it is characteristic of John to assume that people naturally follow their tendencies to extremes. He pictures himself as a conservative but sees in his conservatism

5

certain elements that, blown up, would be fascistic. I remembered his telling me about an article he had read in *Verdict,* a new conservative magazine for students. "It was by a woman who was against teaching children to share their toys. She said it breaks down the idea of private property. Why should one child give his toy to another?"

I laughed, and John, whose tone and manner were usually unrelentingly sincere, let up a bit and conceded, "I know it sounds silly, but still. . . ."

John and I waited outside the restaurant for a table. Three or four professors and several deans passed, recognized John, and spoke to him by name. This was highly unusual. There are more than 25,000 students at the University of Illinois' Champaign campus, and practically all of them could stand outside the Illini Union restaurant for weeks without being recognized by a faculty member. Although he was only a lowly teaching fellow in his first year of graduate studies in the physics department, John was unusual.

He was unusual because he was one of the very few students on the campus who was widely known—by name if not by face —to a large number of his fellow students, to professors, and to administrators. He was known to University officialdom as an embodiment of the academic success story, the young man who went through four undergraduate years in physical engineering with straight A's and then won a Churchill Fellowship for a year's study at Cambridge University. In short, when the University wants to point to its success it points to John and young people like him.

The student body got to know John in his capacity as head of the Conservative Coordinating Council, a very loose coalition of campus conservative groups which, from what John says, are as busy intriguing against each other as they are working for the conservative cause.

It is because John was not typical of the student body, however, that he helped explain it. And to understand the University of Illinois, you must understand this huge mass of undergraduates, the 20,000 of them, who are everywhere, and who, by what they do and by what is done to them, make this place.

John was a loud talker, not a shouter—a loud talker who made it his business to be heard. He did not talk about physics unless you pressed him. What he liked to talk about was his politics, which seemed to serve as a mixture of athletics, religion, and private emotional satisfaction. "The thing that got me interested in politics when I was young, say ten or eleven, was my father and his friends talking about it a lot, so I read newspapers earlier than I would ordinarily. The campus paper here, "DI" [*Daily Illini*], is overwhelmingly one-sided. I hesitate to use the word *liberal,* but it's cynical and left of center. There's a kind of conforming revolt against conformity.

"I watched both conventions on TV in 1960 and the high point was when Goldwater withdrew his name. His speech, the way he said 'Grow up, conservatives!'—it was so authoritative and reasonable and sincere."

John admitted, "I haven't really resolved myself." He tried, however, when he virtually dropped his studies to head the campus Goldwater campaign. For three months he moved in and out of emotional and verbal imbroglios. He looked on it as politics, but it sounded like a period of testing and learning: "On Election Day I was in Chicago getting a brick thrown through my windshield and the air let out of my tires. I was working to keep the vote honest in a precinct in the 27th ward, around Van Buren and Paulina. We argued, the precinct captain and I, all day, sometimes shouting at each other face to face. It started even before the polls were open. So when he started ordering the judges to do this and that, I asked, 'Are you a judge?' and then we went at it, three or four times during the day. I made a scene."

As John recalled his experience, there was a small smile on his usually severe face, like that of a gladiator affectionately remembering an ancient opponent.

7

John admitted that his colleagues at the University hadn't always been sympathetic to his loud conservatism. "There're only two ways to be a conservative in the physics department: you have to be completely quiet or very outspoken. I was outspoken, a rebel. The people in the physics department are very left. I'm unique."

"But if you're a rebel," I asked, "then you're like the left-wing kids you oppose, aren't you?"

"Yes, but conservative rebels tend to be less emotional. We resort to nonactivist-type things. Conservative rebels are clean shaven, and if they're girls, they wear stockings. Our program is strictly educational; we try to bring in speakers for the conservative cause. The conservative rebels' big protest is against the faculty, which is predominantly liberal. We don't protest the way the University is run. Most conservatives agree pretty much with the administration because generally the University is run in a conservative philosophy.

"I had a political science professor who tried to imply Nixon was crooked because he had a $100,000 home. I got up and said that maybe that was because of his being a partner in a big law firm. A lot of students are afraid to say anything in class. I said it and completely ignored what the consequences might be. I got a B in the course. It was a gift. I hadn't studied, but if you're known as a good student, sometimes you'll be graded on your reputation.

"One reason kids don't talk is because they're worried about being humiliated, getting a mocking answer from the teacher. People often aren't aggressive enough.

"It's almost barbarian here. There're more per capita subscriptions to *Playboy* magazine than almost any other place. You see those sorts of magazines on all the racks in the drugstores around campus."

One of the nicest things about this fidgety, energetic, sober-sounding boy was that his life and opinions were impossible to guess in advance. His education had not obliterated a fundamentalist kind of morality; he was genuinely bothered by the Bobby

8

Baker scandal in Washington, by the visible want of personal piety in the nation's leading politicians—and yet there was a visible disgust in John for the religious cant that these politicians pronounce on all suitable public occasions.

His morals have helped make him a conservative. So has his reading of the Constitution, and his discovery that, like fundamentalist morality, the eighteenth-century charter of American liberties is not applied as its writers and signers understood it. In John none of this was a mask for a young man's selfishness. He was not a conservative because he wanted his taxes lowered. In fact, John was poor, and by getting married in his senior year he had made sure that his postgraduate years would be tougher on him than on a single man.

He began to speak of school and marriage: "I looked forward to coming to the University of Illinois so much. I was willing to take the responsibilities that go with it. I never felt homesick till I was married for three weeks. An increasing number of college students are getting married. My parents weren't too happy, but if they'd stopped me there would have been a complete blowup."

For all his success in the earlier stages of becoming a physicist, John Johnson wasn't sure he wanted to be one, and for the multiversity and the society at large this raises some questions. "Physics isn't what it looks like from the outside," he said. "In physics almost every graduate student is subsidized; we are confessed parasites. There's a fantastic amount of waste in science. The reason I ended up in physics [he doesn't say he chose physics] is because every kid in high school who's good at math gets told he is going into science. I was a freshman in high school the year Sputnik went up."

"John, didn't you try to get some counseling when you got here?"

"The counselor in the dorm my freshman year was a law student. He told me I ought to go into law. I went over to the counseling center once, but they said science. I'm thinking about taking some aptitude tests, but I know these tests don't really test aptitudes, and I'll get a high score for science. There's a guy in our office, another graduate student in physics, who's making the decision by committing academic suicide. He's deliberately getting all C's so he'll flunk out of grad school. I think I'd like to switch, probably to economics or something."

After talking to John for three or four hours, I wondered if he really fared better than the thousands of anonymous students on the campus. The faculty and the administration bring him up as an example of institutional success, but is it John they know, or only the name of a young, blue-ribbon academic bull, a boy drafted in his early teens into physics for lifelong service in the scientific side of national defense?

As one of his teachers observed, John is the kind of young man who will be reasonably good at any academic pursuit, but instead of being the capable physicist, could he have made a brilliant social scientist? Moreover, as a physicist, John in years to come may be asked to advise in making political decisions about the application of physics. Will the curious, morally sensitive boy, his real interests blocked, turn into a political eccentric who could be quite dangerous?

John was aware of his teeter-totter position: he had no use for liberals, but the campus John Birch Society was after him as an ideological softie; school had given him precious few tools and little background to use in finding a high, firm ground to stand and think on. He'd had little history as such, that would help him, and when he talked he often fell back on Edmund Burke for a guide.

According to one of its more brilliant members, Professor Herbert J. Muller of the University of Indiana, the multiversity has not seen John's problem and our problem with John. A passage in *The Uses of the Past* begins to make clear just how deep that problem may be:

In our own world, specialization has produced the machine-tender and the bookkeeper, the technician and academician—

the hordes of cultural illiterates and expert ignoramuses. It denies millions the opportunity of really creative work, the elemental satisfaction of saying, "I made this." Even the wealth of opportunities it affords is a wealth of square holes for round pegs; in a civilization [like ours] there are many more possibilities of going wrong, or—as bad—of restless doubts that one has made the best choice. We have innumerable educational agencies for guiding choices of occupation, or for intensifying the confusion by multiplying the possible choices; but we are only beginning to educate for the all-important problem, of coordinating and humanizing our specialized knowledge, bringing our experts together, teaching our technicians to speak a common civilized language.

2

A Bit of Tradition

If you drive to the University of Illinois from Chicago, you come through miles of cornfields, and it's good to remember that the cornfields are important in the University's life. The Illinois Industrial University, as it was known in its early years, apparently was plopped down in an inaccessible field because of an aggressive man named Clark Robinson Griggs. Griggs had made money during the Civil War by selling supplies to the Union Army; in addition to farming at Urbana, Griggs was a railroad promoter, which meant he was a man who knew his way around. Yet with all his talents—he was a state representative from Champaign-Urbana and a well-regarded member of the legislature—Griggs could not have pulled it off if Abraham Lincoln had not signed the Merrill Act of 1862. Under this law every state was given public land, the profits from the sale of which were to be used for "at least one college where the leading object shall be, without excluding other scientific and classical studies, and including military tactics, to teach such branches of learning as are related to agriculture and the mechanic arts. . . ."

There was a catch: the money had to be used within five years of the law's passage or the state lost it. That was all to the good because otherwise Illinois probably would not have been able to pull itself together and establish a state university. Under the Ordinance of 1787—one of the first instances of federal aid to education—Illinois had been given money for a college, or what was then called a "literary institution," but weakness of purpose and the covetous cries of little sectarian colleges like McKendree and Knox resulted in the money being frittered away.

This left the state without a university, although at Bloomington it did have an inadequate institution known as Normal University. Thanks to President Buchanan, who vetoed a federal aid to education bill because he suspected it might be an unconstitutional infringement on state's rights, there was no more money forthcoming from Washington until Lincoln and the Republicans, believers in strong central government, came to power.

Nevertheless, when Griggs set out to bring the University to Champaign-Urbana, he met considerable opposition. The little denominational colleges wanted the money and feared the competition. Places like Chicago, Springfield, and Peoria—with more to recommend them than a remote marsh and a muddy road—wanted the new university, but if they had common sense on their side, they did not have Griggs, who was a tireless, efficient lobbyist for Champaign-Urbana.

The tactics of Griggs at the legislative session of 1867 were calculated to win respect even at a capital where the contemporaries of Lincoln and Douglas had made a fine art of political maneuvering. . . . Spacious quarters were engaged at the largest hotel in Springfield—the Leland; offices, bedrooms, a buffet, and a reception room which held two hundred people. Here he . . . began lobbying on a large scale. Members of either party, hostile or friendly, were invited to the hotel for liquor, for light refreshments, or for huge oyster suppers or quail dinners. They found here a place to lounge in easy chairs, to chat or read newspapers, listen to legislative gossip. . . . They were supplied with cigars, and groups of them were

13

taken to the theater. At the weekends, entertainments of some size were arranged.

In this way, the University of Illinois was built in a cornfield and learned what all state-supported colleges and universities learn: You must make the legislature love you.

On the drive down, however, I did not see the cornfields. They were hidden by a winter mist, and I was too interested in what the other two people in the car were telling me of life at the Champaign campus. The driver of the car was a Presbyterian minister, Larry Hill, and in the back seat was Wally, a very nice but astonishingly fat young man from Monticello, Illinois.

I had met Larry Hill about a year before in the dining car of an Illinois Central train; my newspaper was sending me to cover a big demonstration by northern ministers against Mississippi misgovernment. A round young man with a twinkle, he had grown up in Urbana, where his father is the Champaign County Clerk. He received his bachelor's degree from the University of Illinois, where he had majored in music. Although he at first concentrated on the slide trombone and the cello, he later switched to choral music. About this time he came within the ambit of the Presbyterian Church through the McKinley Foundation, a Tudor pile of bricks right off campus on John Street—one of a number of religious foundations, as they are called at the University of Illinois, that offer chaplaincy services to the student body. Actually they are much more important to the University and the students than that dry description suggests.

It was through McKinley that Larry got his vocational idea of the ministry. Particularly significant was the kind of ministry this young man with a sweet but silly face saw for himself. He became a seeker after "community," a popular term on the campus. People are forever talking about a "community of scholars," the "Christian community," or just the community they are seeking for themselves. The yen, the yearning to place one's self between fixed known points in life, is a powerful tug when the lack of a communal existence is felt so strongly. Though Larry says he switched to choral music because he was a poor musician, I wonder if he did not feel that choral music brought people closer together than other kinds of music in which the instruments and instrumental virtuosity separate them. Choral music, after all, and its ancestor, the chant, are very old forms of communal worship.

The University is so big that there is no possibility of seeing it all yourself. You must see it through other people's eyes—for instance, the eyes of John Johnson and Larry Hill. If John is the morally perturbed young man, jarred by differences between what the adult world professes and what it does, Larry is something of the same. His cure, however, is not John's cure of right thinking and right doing; it is rather a charity, urging Larry to live the life of the least happy, the most pained. It is this charity that led him to Mississippi and turns his thoughts toward Chicago, her Negroes, and her poor.

As we drove along highways that ran southward through fog-hidden fields, plowed and quiet in winter rest, Larry talked about a student who set up a stand to sell Bibles on campus: "The boy was a kind of religious nut. He dropped out of school for a term —I think it was last year—and spent all of his money on Bibles. He set up a little table by the administration building, where he sold them and passed out tracts. The administration told him he couldn't sell the Bibles on University property so he started giving them away. They didn't like that either, said he was littering, and finally they arrested him for trespassing. He had all kinds of Bibles, I mean Bibles in all kinds of languages, and when they arrested him there was a protest demonstration. All the liberal atheists were upset about it and an ACLU lawyer defended him.

"At the trial the administration representative said he was passing out Russian literature. The ACLU lawyer asked him wasn't it true that it was the Bible in Russian, and he answered he didn't know what it said, but he knew it was Russian and that was enough for him." (The University has a Center for Russian Language and Area Studies.)

The talk shifted to the impact of government financing on the University: "We're supposed to have a lot of traditions here—like first homecoming—but it's a bunch of crap. The University has become basically research for the military and defense industries, and in the midst of it the undergraduates are pretty much forgotten. The graduate students do a lot of the teaching, not the professors."

"We get stuck with graduate students who aren't interested," Wally put in. "They just want to get their degrees and $16,000 a year."

I wanted to ask Wally where he thought a young man with a freshly minted Ph.D. could get $16,000 a year starting salary, but he was now well into his own feelings about the students and the school.

"The thing that bothers me is that it's so much like a machine, not only the University but the students too. There aren't 110 of them on our campus who'd even understand why the Berkeley student would want to demonstrate. You have no rights if you're a student. Girls have to be in by a certain time. Freshmen men can't have cars. You either have to live in the dorms or in what is called organized housing, a fraternity, or an organized independent house."

Wally was a young man with freedom on his mind. One of the small band of student brothers who went to Mississippi to work for Negro rights, he was about as atypical of students on the campus as the Bible-seller or John Johnson. Later Larry told me that "Wally had a rough time when he came back from Mississippi. He was resentful of everything. We had a hard time getting him to accommodate himself. He resented the administration and its restraints on the students and he resented the students' indifference. He would hardly talk to anybody who wasn't connected with the civil rights movement."

16

Wally lived in an independent organized house known by the collegiate title of ROOJAH, which stood for Royal Order of Janitors and Hosts. The ROOJAH membership consisted of eight or ten boys who lived in the basement of the McKinley Foundation. Larry was the adult whom the University requires to give such establishments general supervision, which in this case was anything but severe or meddlesome.

Larry remarked that "the students are frantic about their studies," and Martin picked up the thread of the conversation: "It's hell going through now. Lots of people who had no difficulty going through high school have to study all the time. More papers are demanded, their quality has increased, and so the teacher expects you to do more. If you want a good grade, you've got to do more."

It was dark by the time we got to the University. When the public relations office had made a reservation for me at the Student Union, I had been dubious, for the mere name evoked iron bedsteads and communal showers. The Illini Union was nothing of the kind. A monstrous set of Georgian buildings, it had deep-toned wood paneling, carpets and upholstered chairs, and couches with curving legs. We went downstairs almost immediately to have dinner in the Colonial Room, the high-priced restaurant where only faculty and students on a special night out eat.

The Union was a good place to learn certain things about the University. The lounges conveyed the University mood of work; although presumably designed as places of conversation, there was little talk in them. All day long, from quite early in the morning until quite late in the evening, the occupied hush of study dominated. When I asked the students why they studied there, I almost always received one of two answers: "My dorm's too noisy. I can't study there," or, "My dorm's too far away. By the time I'd get back to my room I'd have to leave for class again."

The menu at the restaurant that night represented the fusion of two drives which operated on the campus. The first was generated by well-intentioned faculty wives or World Federalist groups working for international understanding; the second, by an ubiquitous urge to foster culture and provide what everybody called "opportunities" for students and faculty alike. The meal consisted entirely of South American dishes—things like Brazilian codfish balls—inedible but in keeping with "International Week" at the Union, when foods and native handicrafts from around the world are exhibited.

For our South American dinner we sat with a young anthropologist and his date, a thin girl of long, dark hair, an art student. The anthropologist, fresh from an Ivy League university, was in a supercilious mood: "You don't know about the three-week rule? Well, let me tell you," he warned, "if you're in a fraternity and you date a sorority girl (the students at the University claim that there are more fraternities and sororities here than on any other campus) for three weeks, you're entitled to a kiss."

"Sometimes it's just the second date," the girl corrected him.

"Well, whatever it is, they have strict rules for it. Social custom is law here, as it is with societies we insist on calling 'underdeveloped.' When the girls come back to the sororities after their dates, they have a ritual in the living room. They turn off all the lights, hold candles and chant."

"They only do it with the pledges," the girl said gently.

"Yes, yes, with the pledges. They surround her and chant, 'Oh, now you must tell, oh, now you must tell.' "

"Tell what?" I wanted to know.

"Well, whatever happened on the date, like getting pinned."

(Being "pinned" means being given a fraternity pin by your boyfriend. The DI carries a regular feature called "The Party Line," which announces the week's lavalierings, pinnings, engagements, and marriages. The least frequent, and apparently the least binding, is being "lavaliered," that is, being given a necklace with your boyfriend's fraternity insignia attached. Some of the rakish male spirits are said to borrow pins from their fraternity brothers so they can pin more than one girl at a time. Girls have also been said to accept more than one pin at a time, but these forms of collegiate polygamy and polyandry are both rare and disapproved of, according to most of the people I talked to.)

"It does serve some purpose, of course," the anthropologist went on. "These little girls are here out of the bosoms of their homes for the first time in their lives. They need friends, need to establish relationships, so they're pledged in these sororities that have these weird, sentimental ceremonies to make them feel even more morose, and then they turn on the lights and clasp the new members to their breasts and the new ones look around at their 'sisters' and say, 'Oh, isn't it just wonderful, these girls are just like me!' "

"They keep them busy; God, I'll say that for them," the girl said. "D'you know about 'activity points?' "

"No."

"When they're pledges, more or less on probation, one of the ways they have to prove themselves is by how many activities they get into. They have to get so many points. It can be for anything—student government, Star Course [the name of the student organization, dominated by the Greeks, that arranges concerts on campus for performers who range from Harry Belafonte to Artur Rubinstein], the DI, or helping blind old ladies across the street."

(I learned in the course of my visit that the cutting young anthropologist was not always accurate in what he told me. The facts, and what the students think are the facts, often are at variance, but it is such talk that freshmen hear and from it shape their picture of the school. In the confusion of people, rules, buildings, and new strains of one's first days on campus it is often the chance remark of some particularly vivid speaker that sinks the deepest. Moreover, unless the misinformation is about a topic in which you are particularly interested, you may not bother to get the facts—you could sail through four undergraduate years imagining that every pledge is driven in everything he does by an insatiate desire to collect activity points. The Greeks I talked to didn't have activity points in their houses, but they'd heard of them.)

"It's cannibalistic ritual, a lot of it. Like Wednesday night exchanges. You can stand outside any fraternity and see them emerge, by order of height, smallest to the largest, and go, troop, troop, troop over to a sorority, and there they pair up with the girls who are waiting for them in order of height. They'll dance or sing or something, and bring the girls back to their house, and off they go, troop, troop, troop, back to their own house."

Not all anthropologists looking at the American campus have been satisfied with making flip remarks. Some have put the tools of a trade we are used to seeing applied to Fiji Islanders to work at understanding what they call "the academic culture." At Champaign-Urbana, as an anthropologist might see it, the academic culture is made up of two different societies: the dominant faculty and subordinate student body.

The past and present are loaded with examples of bigger and lesser societies bumping into each other like the Romans and Germanic barbarians, cowboys and Indians, Peace Corps men and natives of Borneo. The dominant society teaches the subordinate society, but the lessons are sometimes learned in strange ways. Faculty and undergraduates at Illinois are, in a certain sense, members of different societies, with different ways of doing things, different social arrangements and subgroupings, and different values.

An instructor of hematology, most of whose days are spent trying to learn new things about blood chemistry, lives in a different universe from the young lady in his class who is taking notes to pass an exam so she can be a lab technician of a routine sort. Outside the classroom, teachers have committee meetings, academic politics, research, their professional associations to occupy them; undergraduates have dorms, fraternities, a vastly different social and intellectual life.

The student society on the receiving end, though usually submissive, does resist sometimes by refusing to learn all that the faculty teaches, sometimes by secretly not playing the faculty's rules—perhaps cheating, for example. Then there are the times when the two societies break into open hostilities, as occurred at Yale and Berkeley. Guerilla warfare is much more common but seldom comes to light. When it does, it is by a fluke, like the discovery of cheating rackets at the Air Force Academy.

3

The Idea Is to Pass

A first-year graduate student in the English Department, Richard Traver already had something of the look of the high-powered intellectual about him. There were blotchy red spots on his roundish face, his glasses tended to slide down his nose, and every morning he could be found in the basement cafeteria under the Illini Union, eating a small breakfast in the company of a protégé and an attaché case.

The protégés seemed to change almost daily. The attaché case contained everything Richard needed—books, papers, articles—as though each dawn he provisioned it with not only the day's study materials, but supporting documentation for upcoming casual conversations, as well as items of educational value for his friends. Happily, he was more interested in spreading ideas than in showing off. When he asked, "Did you read Harold Taylor's symposium?" and I admitted I hadn't, he pulled out a copy from the attaché case.

Richard had been an editor of DI, with the result that, like John Johnson and the Bible salesman, he was another of those rare people on campus whose names were known. In Richard's case, the name he had made came not from occupying a position, but from what he did with the position—which was to become a nervy critic who did well at unnerving the administration. He attacked the administration for its policies on academic freedom, on rules for undergraduates, on the quality of the education being handed out to the students, on everything; since he wrote well, what he said hurt.

Now Richard was enraged over the University's decision to build an intramural athletic building. It was to cost about six million dollars and be paid for by student fees of between ten and fifteen dollars a semester. Richard and the liberal and radical groups on campus had a raft of objections: the added cost would make it more difficult for poorer students to attend the University; there were already extra fees and charges that had to be paid above room, board, and tuition. Dorm space, particularly housing for married students, was needed more. The Intramural Department was trying to build an empire for itself. Since the students would have to pay for the building, they should decide if they want it; instead of giving them that chance, the administration had acted underhandedly by taking a group of students designated as "representative leaders" on a free airplane ride and fun trip to a number of Big Ten campuses, ostensibly to let them see other new IMA buildings, but really to bribe them into supporting the idea. (Needless to say, the administration, while conceding the airplane ride—but not the opponents' version of what it was for—has an answering argument for all the charges.)

I asked Richard about the "Slob Contingent," a group of graduate and undergraduate students described to me as hanging suspended in a jelly of discontent and disappointment.

"You're in luck. They're in the next room, the Tavern."

The Tavern was also cafeteria style but, unlike the big common cafeteria in the strictly institutional Union basement, was outfitted as Ye Olde English Tavern. The chairs were more comfortable, and the illumination came from large yellow glass fixtures, barrel-shaped and trimmed with what I took to be Tudor-style, wrought-iron trim. A jukebox, in operation at all

23

times, played a loud assortment of rock 'n' roll numbers that were indistinguishable from each other.

The Slob Contingent got its name from a letter in the DI complaining of its invariable presence in the Tavern and urging that the management take steps to throw out this bunch of lounging, coffee-drinking students. The Slob Contingent claimed that the management had already tried such artful devices as increasing the wattage in the Tavern's lights and closing the room down several times a day for brief periods of cleaning.

(American college educators have always wanted their charges to act like perfect little gentlemen. The Statutes of Harvard College, written about 1646, state that the students "shall be slow to speak, and eschew not only oaths, lies and uncertain rumors, but likewise all idle, foolish, bitter scoffing, frothy wanton words and offensive gestures.")

In the Tavern, Richard introduced me to Catherine. Despite her collegiate style—green sweater, rust slacks cut along the lines of ski pants, soft freckles, and hair piled loosely on top of her head—she had an older woman's anxiety and tension. She said she was twenty-one but the way she talked was not youth's confidence but the opinionated voice of a person who has had the wrong kinds of involved and insoluble emotional problems. Sometimes Catherine's youth would show in her conversation, through gaps in her knowledge or awkwardness, but most of the time she spoke as though she had been overused and badly used. She seemed to be disgusted with herself for seeking knowledge, disgusted with her fellow students for diploma chasing, and disgusted with the University for thinking it might be a center of high culture and learning.

"Underlying all that is wrong about this place," she told me, "is that nothing can be done about it."

I asked her to tell me a little of her history.

"I'm from Philadelphia. My father's an electrical engineer. I went to an exclusive prep school, the kind where if you do under 650 in your college boards, you're an idiot. When I was a senior in high school I wanted to revolutionize twentieth-century thought, and then I discovered I couldn't do mathematics. [The University requires a certain amount of math in the liberal arts curriculum.] Probably I shouldn't have come here. I made a mistake when I was in high school. There was a feeling we all had about getting away from Philadelphia, away from the Ivy League, a feeling for the Middle West and the land."

"Crap," commented a young man at the round table where we were sitting.

"No, I still get the feeling sometimes. Do you know this is the richest farmland in the world? All that corn—they make everything and grow everything out here. When I came here I thought it would do something for me, I didn't know what, and I had the idea you attack philosophy, that it was something you read and discussed. I thought at long last this was the begining of learning. . . ."

Catherine's observation was one I was to hear often from the brightest liberal arts students; they had come seeking a beginning to learning, and had found themselves in a sort of continuation of high school, with rules, rote memorizing, and "do it because I tell you to do it—you'll understand why later." They seemed to provide considerable confirmation to David Riesman's remark: "Many colleges are now in effect in the same position that many high schools have been in for some time, that is, of being cram schools for the next stage."

Why had she picked the University of Illinois?

"It wasn't the 'college of my choice' [a universal phrase on application forms, and often spoken in irony by students], Reed [Oregon] was. I was admitted there, but I didn't get a scholarship and it cost too much for me to go without one. Anyway, the University of Illinois had a good reputation, not that anybody in the high school really knew much about it."

(Riesman and others have long complained about the mismating of students and college: "There are hardly any policies for getting the right teachers and students to the right colleges, and then to the right classrooms." Nor is installing a "guidance counselor" in a high school any assurance, since no one really knows what is the "right" college for a given sort of person. An additional problem is that so much information about college is inaccurate or out of date. Nor does sticking with name brands necessarily help because, as Riesman says, "Among the well-established colleges, the alumni are probably the group who do most to determine the brand-name image, and to keep it a generation out of date.")

In Catherine's case, the pitch of the place seemed wrong; she felt it pushed her toward learning, not for its own sake, but to train her to do a job. She was under the influence of philosophy's great tradition of unifying knowledge and drawing meaning from human experience, but philosophy at the University was not taught, she complained, in the grand tradition, but was directed at turning out philosophers—careerists with degrees and technical proficiency in logic. The classroom treatment of Aristotle's politics was not the quest for truth, she said, and the professor made no effort to relate it to modern political problems.

"Isn't that your job?" I asked. "Isn't the quest for truth as much your responsibility as the teacher's?"

She considered the idea, then gave it a mild assent. It was my first brush with an attitude I was to find among many of the brighter students—the assumption that, as in learning technique ("five finger exercises" one of the professors would call it), you could be passive and absorb an education by memorizing the right material.

"I know," she said. "You can't have just one person responding in a classroom and everybody else scribbling notes. One day Dr. Diggs [B. J. Diggs, chairman of the Philosophy Department] really started talking to us about ethics—the way you can talk about ethics if you're eighty years old or a philosopher. He was talking about 'is' and 'ought,' the heart of ethics. I could tell he wanted us to talk and ask questions, and all you could hear were students' pens scratching notes. Toward the end of the class, it was silent in the room; he was waiting for us to talk, but we didn't. When the bell rang, Dr. Diggs left.

"I had a young English teacher; he'd just come here, and he was full of enthusiasm for English and teaching it. A very good teacher who wanted to work with the students. He'd have coffee and doughnuts for students in his office and in class he'd say again and again, 'Come to my office, come to my office,' but nobody ever did. After a while he got disgusted and stopped trying. He was still a good teacher, but the hope he had at the beginning was gone; he was appalled by our inarticulateness.

"We can be very self-centered; not selfish, but self-centered. During the Cuban missile crisis some of the girls were running all over the dorm eating food because they thought they wouldn't get any more. That's all some of them were thinking of.

"They go to school in the same self-centered way—not for knowledge, not to learn. The two questions I've heard the most often are, 'Will it be on the final exam?' and if they see you're reading a book, they ask, 'Are you reading it for a course?' That's the only reason they read a book. The instructors are the same way. Ask them about the subject and they say 'Don't worry about it. It won't be on the final exam.' The idea is to pass, not learn."

Nobody seems to know what the "idea"—that is, the purpose —of college really is. Riesman, who does not write to shock, suggests that, beyond the usual reasons advanced in defense of post high school education, "The American college exists as a vast WPA project, which gives promising adolescents work to do while keeping them out of the job market, and also keeping several hundred thousand faculty members off the streets."

Once upon a time the American college was able, almost with one voice, to say what the idea was. What has become known as "The Yale Report of 1828" carefully laid down what should be taught in college and why. For nearly fifty years it served as *the* creed of liberal arts education as the American college came under increasing attack for its refusal to teach less Latin and Greek and more science. Since 1828, American educators have made an infinite number of statements in defense of the liberal arts, the classic curriculum, and against using the college for vocational training, but the argument was made first and best by Yale:

> What then is the appropriate object of a college? . . . its object is to *lay the foundation of a superior education:* and this is to be done, at a period of life when a substitute must be provided for *parental superintendence.* The ground work of a thorough education, must be broad, and deep, and solid.
>
> The two great points to be gained in intellectual culture are the *discipline* and the *furniture* of the mind; expanding its powers, and storing it with knowledge. . . .
>
> But why, it may be asked, should a student waste his time upon studies which have no immediate connection with his future profession? . . . In answer to this, it ought to be observed that there is no science which does not contribute its aid to professional skill. "Everything throws light upon everything." The great objection of a collegiate education, preparatory to the study of a profession, is to give that expansion and balance of the mental powers, those liberal and comprehensive views, and those fine proportions of character which are not to be found in him whose ideas are always confined to one particular channel. . . .

Yale and liberal arts lost the battle, perhaps the bitterest that has ever divided American schoolmen. A century later, people would say that colleges which teach liberal arts only do so because they don't have the money to pay for the labs and for the professors who can offer a modern curriculum.

The disappearance of the classic curriculum inherited from the late Middle Ages and the Renaissance has, however, made the purpose of college education more obscure. In the old days, everybody agreed that learning Latin, mathematics, and philosophy was "broadening" (a word often used and seldom defined); by the early 1920's, however, colleges and universities were talking about training people for specific kinds of work: you learned chemistry, not to be broadened, but to be a chemist.

An undergraduate at the University of Illinois may take courses —for credit—in saleswriting, horse production, aircraft shop practice, advanced typewriting, dairy cattle judging, and life insurance. The Department of Health and Safety Education offers courses in first aid and advanced traffic safety education. The Department of Home Economics has a course called "Clothing Selection," and a "clothing laboratory" (Home Economics 182), which delves into the "fitting problems in the selection of ready-to-wear." Another, offered in alternate years to juniors and seniors only, is called "Restaurant Interiors." It is "designed to give the student information and vocabulary necessary to work intelligently with professional decorators."

When Catherine said, "the idea is to pass, not learn," she was criticizing, but many students, as the catalogue shows, may not be studying subjects really worth "learning" in an academic sense, and so may be in a position where the only sensible thing is to concentrate on passing. In actuality, passing may be the whole and sole reason for a course. Riesman suspects as much when thinking about premed work: "Two years of 'majoring' may be just an extended medical aptitude test. Indeed, some professors of medicine urge this view, saying that they have to teach all the required scientific material over again in medical school anyway, and that the only point of undergraduate requirements is to allow the medical schools to reject misfits instead of having them flunk out."

Medical schools do have lower flunk-out rates than other kinds of postgraduate schools, and since it is cheaper to reject a student beforehand than to let him in and flunk him out later, an undergraduate obstacle course may pay off for the medical school. Whether it pays off for the college, whether it helps create the kind of student Catherine is talking about—the kind who learns how to pass and not much else—is another matter.

Some students do not even have the solace of looking forward to a brighter academic future when they will be expected to learn as well as pass; some are studying professions that really don't exist. The most frequently cited example is the business school. Since it is impossible to know what "business" is, it is impossible to think up a course of training for it. "Thus," Riesman notes, "courses in business law often are more a laying on of hands to reassure students that they have learned something real than any introduction to the legal problems a businessman might confront. As a result, many undergraduate schools of business, despite the courses in marketing, production control, and so on, have in effect transformed themselves into second-rate departments of economics, with a smattering of social science and writing courses thrown in. . . . Unfortunately for the students, many personnel offices have discovered this, and increasingly prefer liberal arts graduates who are likely to be more sophisticated."

State-supported schools are all too willing to please ambitious occupational groups who hope to get into the social register of the professions by getting into a university catalogue. And there is money in it, for both the trade and the university. Any trade that can, like medicine, limit the number of practitioners by insisting they have special initials after their names, can control prices as well as raise its social standing. Every additional group lobbying for the state university in the legislature helps to win a larger appropriation—and push up the cost of education.

Despite the existence of such courses as "Restaurant Interiors," Catherine made it clear that Illinois is not an easy school. "It's difficult to get A's here. They make it hard in petty ways. PE— physical education—is a good example. I'm not against exercise. We're fat and flabby. Our diet is cokes, french fries, and hamburgers unless you eat in the dorms, ugh, so I don't mind taking ice skating, but why do they have to try to teach us to be Olympic ice skaters? It's stupid. I flunked volleyball. We had to take a written examination on the international, official volleyball rules, or whatever they call them. And I flunked. It's stupid.

"That's one reason I flunked out. I'm not sure they would actually flunk you out if you were doing all right in everything else, but it pushed me over."

"How did you get back?" I wanted to know.

"I was out of school for about a year, lived in Chicago and audited courses at the University of Chicago. Then I petitioned to come back. I explained I'd become more mature in the meantime." Catherine made her contempt clear when she said "more mature."

After agreeing to meet Catherine later, I set out for the married student housing compound. I had been told that there was to be a meeting there because the students were worried that their cheap, university-supplied housing was to be torn down. The compound was immediately recognizable—frame cabins, known as "prefabs," that were covered with asphalt shingle or siding. This line of prefabs was called Stadium Terrace because it sat across the street from the football field with its high-banked tiers of seats, intimidatingly large when empty.

By contrast the prefabs looked like miniatures. In front of the tiny houses were small fences and the debris of children's play—a dismantled tricycle, a rusting part of a play gun. The children themselves were inside for the winter.

Graduate students and graduate studies have not always been part of American higher education. The first earned Ph.D. was awarded by Yale in 1861, and even that was tainted in that the Yale of that era had no graduate school, or at least none that we would recognize today.

In those days, the Ph.D. degree, an as-yet unpopularized German import, was hardly known. The master's degree was known and given, but it did not mean much since, to qualify, about all you had to do was stay in school and out of jail. In 1842, Francis Wayland, the president of Brown, was moved to say of the M.A., "As it is now, to all practical purposes, we throw this degree away. . . . The best and the worst scholars are equally entitled to it on the third year after graduation."

31

They continued to throw it away, although American school-men, especially from the 1840's on, agitated for one real university—that is, an institution that taught students who had already received their B.A.'s. One of the most articulate agitators was Henry P. Tappan, who devoted most of his life to replicating in the United States German universities like Heidelberg or Gottingen.

Tappan's book *University Education* was a major propaganda statement for the Prussian educational system. In his attack on the American college and in his expression of hope for the future, it is just possible to discern graduate students living in prefabs, serving small-pay apprenticeships:

> . . . . education has become superficial by attempting too much in the short period allotted [to the four year college]. . . . We have called our colleges universities; we have tried to enlarge our course of studies more and more; we seem to have been struggling to afford every imaginable facility; and yet we have only a superficial and inadequate education.
>
> . . . . we must do something besides multiplying colleges after the same model, pouring forth a tide of school books, and making experiments upon a facile system of education full of pretension and fair promises. . . .
>
> The establishment of Universities in our country will reform . . . our educational system. By the Universities we mean such . . . where study may be extended without limit, where the mind may be cultivated according to its wants and where . . . the bauble of an academical diploma is forgotten.

Tappan was offered the presidency of the University of Michigan, and in 1852 he went to Ann Arbor to make a university. He failed. Michigan wanted immediately useful knowledge for its farms and factories, not the impracticalities of Tappan's abstruse graduate school scholarship. His graduate school does not seem to have enrolled more than ten students, and Tappan himself was increasingly criticized, not only for his educational ideas, but also for such suspect personal habits as taking wine at dinner.

Other attempts to introduce graduate education were made—at Columbia, Rochester, Pennsylvania, and elsewhere. All were unsuccessful. Then in 1876 something happened which was as important to America as John D. Rockefeller's creation of Standard Oil: Johns Hopkins University, the first big producer of Ph.D.'s in the United States, opened its doors. In fact, the American corporation and this new type of American university have an intertwined history. They began about the same time. At first, the university was dependent on the corporation—in the person of such major benefactors as Vanderbilt, Rockefeller (the University of Chicago), and Leland Stanford. Today, however, as Berelson has pointed out, the corporations are almost completely dependent on the universities for their indispensable professional personnel: "The organization in this country that employs most Ph.D.'s today is not Harvard or Yale or Illinois or Michigan. It is Du Pont. Furthermore, General Electric has more than twice as many Ph.D.'s on its staff as Princeton, Shell has more than MIT, Union Carbide or Eastman or IBM has about as many as Northwestern or Cal Tech. . . . The federal government has more than any of these, about as many as the top 10 universities put together."

Johns Hopkins University was founded on the profits Mr. Hopkins had garnered from the Baltimore and Ohio Railroad. The donor himself knew no more than that he wanted a university. It was left to Daniel Coit Gilman (1831-1908), the University's first president, to build the new institution into what it became. It was he who organized and recruited the teachers and students, then ran the school during its epochal years. He built existing ideas and precedents into a workable system. The end result, a research institution of publishing scholars, became *the* model and *the* standard of American academic quality as Johns Hopkins' Ph.D.'s left the mother graduate school to emulate it at dozens of universities across the land.

33

If what Gilman did at Johns Hopkins is not exactly the life of hard-up graduate students living in cast-off army houses across the street from a large football stadium, his description of his accomplishments, written in 1902, clearly foreshadows the present:

Investigation has . . . been among us the duty of every learned professor, and he has been guide and inspirer of fellows and pupils, whose work may not bear his name, but whose results are truly products of the inspiration and guidance which he has freely bestowed. [Today, one of the graduate students' most frequent complaints is that supervising professors steal the students' original research work and publish it under their own names—sometimes giving the student no more acknowledgement than the typist.]

. . . . a system of fellowships, of scholarships, and of other provisions for advanced study was established here, so well adapted to the wants of the country at that time that its provisions have been widely copied in other places. [Most full-time graduate students still get fairly sizeable help if only in the form of teaching fellowships. Unlike college education, graduate schools —excluding law and medicine—have never been able to attract a significant number of students who can pay their own way.]

It now seems as if there was a danger of rivalry in the solicitation of students, which is unworthy. . . . [The danger Gilman foresaw is a reality: universities now bid for promising graduate students.]

When this university began, the opportunities for scientific publication in this country were very meagre. . . . This university . . . determined to establish certain journals which might be the means of communication between scholars. . . . Three journals were soon commenced: the American Journal of Mathematics; the American Journal of Philology; the American Chemical Journal. . . . Generous encouragement was given to the publication of important treatises. [There are now so many Ph.D.'s being hatched annually—the yearly extrusion rate is about 14,000—that it is a distinction to have your Ph.D. thesis published, so much so that young Ph.D.'s have been known to subsidize publication out of their own pockets.]

I am not without apprehensions that our example to the country has been infelicitous, not less than thirty institutions being known to me, which are now engaged in the work of publication.

Today the standard of judgment of a university is the quality of its graduate schools and the research they do, but the system of truly higher education initiated by Gilman did not take the American campus by storm. Henry Seidel Canby's description of the situation at Yale in the 1890's suggests how gradual its acceptance was: "Around the college had grown up in the latter nineteenth century a haphazard, ill-balanced collection of professional schools, attended by hard-working meagre creatures with the fun drained out of them, who were looked upon with suspicion by the undergraduates, since few of them had been graduated from our college. . . . The university . . . was in my day [the 1890's] a parasite sucking for its own excellent purposes the blood of the college, or more accurately, of that college life which engendered the loyalty of gift-giving alumni."

In some ways the observation is still quite valid. Graduate education is still parasitical in that it costs much more to provide per pupil than does undergraduate education; Seymour Harris has explained, however, that it brings in huge sums in grants and research contracts. Graduate students still are "hard-working meagre creatures," not really students, not really faculty members, enduring today's pittances for tomorrow's rewards, an isolated group without a proper social place—5,000 out of 25,000 students at Champaign, living in trailers or far out on the campus circumference in "married-student housing."

The meeting was to be held in a prefab that had been made over into a small community center. The graduate student wives moved toward the meeting, in rumpled cotton dresses with coats

35

thrown over their shoulders, carrying babies. I fell in with one who handed me her baby to carry. Her husband was working for a Ph.D. in English.

"I don't know what we'll do if the University tears these houses down. I know they don't look like much from the outside, but they're quite nice inside—I mean they keep them up. We don't have any hope of getting as much for the money we're paying ($60 a month for four rooms, all utilities). The University's built new married-student housing, but it costs about double this rent."

"And you can't have a washer in the apartment. They told us that would be an extravagance," the wife of a metallurgy student chimed in. "We bought one for $25—secondhand, of course. My husband put a new pump in it, and it's worked fine. Why, for a family with a couple of children to go to the laundromat would cost, my God, about $30 a month!"

The first wife, whose husband, by teaching or research, made between two thousand and twenty-four hundred dollars in a nine-month academic year, said, "We all have to live on substandard incomes, so we expect to live in substandard housing. I don't want you to think we're asking for luxuries."

When they were more or less assembled—perhaps forty of them on folding metal chairs—a graduate student, whose fine features reminded one of an especially well-drawn picture of a young Arab, opened the meeting. His name was Victor Cleron, and he was getting his Ph.D. in Chemistry. Under any circumstances he wouldn't have looked old enough to be twenty-six and the father of two children, but as he began to speak he seemed much younger. His shirt collar was so big that his tie couldn't close the gap; his manner of speaking was academic and halting, betraying him as someone who had never practiced the political arts.

"I—ah—I think we ought to keep in mind what, the—ah—goals, of our group are. They are three in number. One, to keep the prefabs up, and two, I suppose, is—ah—the research function, talking to architects, engineers gathering facts, and the third would be keeping this before the—ah—public."

He and another young man took turns in reviewing what had been transacted between them and the University. They talked about "setting up a dialogue with the University," and were smarting over University Provost Lyle Lanier's having described them as "an idiosyncratic group," the academic bureaucracy's expression for a bunch of crackpots. (Lanier was described as the number two man in the administration, second only to David Dodds Henry, the president.)

There were two guest speakers. One was Roy D. Murphy, an architect with a bashed-in boxer's face and an unpoised way of speaking. Murphy was more than an architect: he was also a builder and an entrepreneur with hopes of building married-student housing in the right price range. Private-enterprise dorm building on campuses is threatening to become a big business across the country. He told the students it was better to have free enterprise build their houses for them, showed them a sketch of what he might be able to do for them, spoke vaguely about what the rentals might be, and then suggested that there would be a happy ending for everyone if the students would use whatever leverage they had to get the University to give him land cheap, or even free.

A second guest was State Representative Jerry Scariano. A small man in a buff-colored corduroy suit, he talked to the students in a low, somewhat halting way, all the while clasping his hands in front of his stomach. There was a doubting, almost jesting note to his voice as he said, "It's really heartening to learn that private enterprise is interested. But I'm not too optimistic. In my opinion there are very few problems in state government that can't be solved with money and I don't think this is one of the few. The question is, are we going to get the money?

"I don't think we're going to find anything for student housing in the budget the University'll bring into the legislature. I'm really not hopeful that anybody in the administration is going to do something. . . . Of course some of us know where to look in the budget for money that's not being used.

"One of the things we might have to do is convince the University that this is at least as important as athletics. They need another athletic field around here as much as I need fleas." (This last, of course, was a reference to the IMA building.)

"What can we do to show this is a state problem?" a student wife asked Scariano.

"You can always buttonhole your representatives and senators. This should help since you're from many parts of the state. They're going to say, 'How does Senator Peters feel about this,' and if he's against you, you aren't going to have much of a chance." (Peters is the local State Senator, who is not only a spokesman for the University but also one of the main powers in running it.)

Scariano went on with his lesson in applied political science: "Don't send petitions to legislators. Everybody's always shoving petitions in front of their noses. Send letters, that will help do the trick. I do think the University will have to do something if it wants to attract good graduate students."

A student said from his seat: "Well, they claim the University wants more advanced students. . . ."

Another student wanted to know, "If we get a dialogue going with the administration, and we're meeting with them, won't that help?"

"Yes," Scariano said, "I think we can solve this if we have a dialogue with the administration, but right now I'm not so sure we're having one."

By prearrangement, I met Catherine again and she took me to visit Meg Bart, an assistant in the English Department, one of the dozens who teach the freshman rhetoric course. Like physical education, it is required of all entering students; it is the only purely academic course that every undergraduate must take, whether he majors in aviation or zoology. "It's the flunk-out course," Catherine said.

"What do you mean by 'flunk-out course'?"

"It's supposed to flunk out about half the entering freshmen. They don't have the space for them, a lot of them really can't do the work, so they use this course to flunk them out."

"Do you realize you're saying that a great university like this has actually designed a course not to teach, but to do the opposite, that is, drive students away from learning. I doubt that."

"That's what Rhet 101 is for. Look, this is a state university, and the law here says they have to take any graduate of any Illinois high school. If you come back in the second semester you'll see whole dorms closed."

At the apartment where we met Meg, Catherine continued to elaborate her flunk-out course thesis, but Meg, a shy young woman needing repeated assurances that her name wouldn't be used, quietly disagreed. "The students here feel the University is really out to get them," she said, speaking as though picking out dry spots in a muddy field to walk on. "Only five kids raised their hands when I asked them how many would take Rhet 101 if they didn't have to. This is the most rebellious student body I've ever seen."

(Meg should see Berkeley—she came here from a small southern college and Illinois by contrast is rebellious. Catherine, from a different background, which includes a sojourn at the University of Chicago, sees the students as horribly docile. Taken as a whole, the American higher educational system is indescribably varied, so that when people from different parts of it, with different experiences, arrive on the same campus they see the same thing differently.)

Catherine was not appeased. "Let me tell you what the course is like. Three spelling errors and you get an automatic C. Three punctuation errors, another automatic C."

"The department does that," Meg explained, "so that all the Rhet sections will have the same standards."

"This is a wonderful place for learning how to live with the bureaucracy," Catherine commented.

(One of the University's many publications listed more than 130 assistants in English, all or most of whom were teaching the Rhet courses. Richard told me that the English Department customarily drafted faculty wives into as many of these positions as possible. That way, after the first semester cutdown in freshmen, the University did not have to pay the salaries of assistants who no longer had classes to teach.)

As Meg described the Rhet course, I could only think of her as light doing battle with darkness, a frail warrior of refinement and civilization tussling with ignorant barbarism: "You just don't have any idea how students in the course can't do the work. They can't spell, they can't punctuate, they can't write a paragraph, they can't think, can't put their thoughts together.

"If a paragraph is supposed to be a coherent theme—say a student's supposed to write about Joe's apartment—they'll give a theme about Joe's life history or the janitor of the building. You have to teach them to think—that's what this course really does. . . . Give them an assignment to help them learn to think, like writing an analogy, and they'll come up with the weirdest things, like comparing a train wreck to a football game."

Meg's nervousness grew as she talked. She fidgeted with cigarettes, went out of the room for coffee, asked again that her name not be used, and finally simply vanished. Catherine and I left to make a tour of the student bierstubes.

They had little of the legendary student drinking places about them. If the students still sing their drinking songs, they didn't that night. The music was being supplied by a plangent rock 'n' roll jukebox.

Catherine said many of the students were under Illinois' legal drinking age, an observation that was repeated to me many times by students, faculty, and administration. Most people assumed that the University knew this and tolerated it. One administrator told me that the enforcement of the drinking laws was the responsibility of the City of Champaign.

While we drank our coffee, I asked Catherine if the drinking ever led to fighting. Catherine said that it sometimes did. I didn't put much store by her remark; with so many thousands of young people living in such close quarters, often under extreme tension, fighting might occasionally take place anywhere. A day or so later I picked up the *Daily Illini* and read:

Five Men Arrested. . . .

STUDENT STABBED IN FIGHT SATURDAY

Champaign police arrested five men Sunday while investigating a fight that led to the stabbing of a University student late Saturday night.

The article then described where the incident had occurred—a student bar five or six hundred feet from the Administration building.

A few days earlier the *Daily Illini* had printed an article on the Faculty Senate Subcommittee on Undergraduate Discipline. It read in part: "One student was placed on conduct probation for violation of the state liquor laws and disorderly conduct. A student who violated state liquor laws [transportation of liquor with a broken seal] was placed on conduct probation. . . . One student was given a reprimand of record for violation of state liquor laws [under-age drinking]."

Stabbings are rare, but such fracases as these are as much a part of undergraduate life as infinite regress is part of mathematics. The riots at Fort Lauderdale are another subject altogether. Some college students may go wild there just because they cannot (or do not) do so at school. What is pretty certain, however, is that the fathers, grandfathers, and even the great-grandfathers of this college generation were not ideal examples for their nose-to-the-grindstone progeny.

One piece of evidence, published in 1911, is a racy pamphlet,

The Demoralization of College Life. It is the work of a Boston journalist hired by a Chicago businessman named Crane, who thought colleges were bad places for good kids. It contains sensational accounts of riots and debauchery, and the reporter even includes an arresting bit of sociological quantification:

> I am able to give you the following estimates, which I believe hit the nail on the head and should now put you on sure footing. These figures, I believe, are accurate as any figures could be, short of two or three years of the most painstaking investigation.
>
> On the basis of 100 students:
> That drink liquor of some kind in freshman year ... 90 percent
> That drink liquor of some kind in senior year ...... 95 percent
> That combine, to a mild degree, wine and bad
> women .... 65 percent
> That drink heavily .... 35 percent
> That have two or three "bats" a year also .... 45 percent
> That go irretrievably to the bad (drunkards) ...... 15 percent

Our next stop was more of a faculty-graduate student bar, where by unwritten agreement the area right of the door was reserved for the University's homosexual colony, there apparently not being enough of them to support a bar of their own. Toward the rear, safely in heterosexual territory, Richard was softly presiding over a conversation about a Japanese math teacher who liked to teach his students to play a game called "Go," roughly describable as a kind of surrealistic checkers. There was more conversation than in the undergraduate tavern. Combined with the jukebox, it made it hard to get people's names straight. Richard was talking to a math department assistant named Ken Bowan; the pretty young woman at his side turned out to be his wife, Johanna.

Richard introduced the subject of universities stealing each other's teachers: "Teachers don't come here to stay. This is a place where they make their reputation and move. I have an

English professor whom you should meet—he just got an offer from the University of Virginia. They wanted him so badly they offered to give his daughter's boyfriend an assistantship to get him there. This business of a university building up a department by raiding another campus for top men—it's all over, not just at Illinois."

This kind of academic brigandage is nothing new in American higher education. Perhaps its most celebrated practitioner was the University of Chicago's William Rainey Harper. In the early 1890's this "captain of erudition" made a descent on Clark University. With money from Rockefeller and a persuasive tongue, Harper made off with half of Clark's academic staff, including fifteen professors.

G. Stanley Hall, Clark's president, left a firsthand account which could easily be updated:

> President Harper of the University of Chicago appeared on the scene. He had made many proposals to eminent men to join his staff but they had been turned down because of a critical attitude toward a "Standard-Oil institution" . . . but . . . Dr. Harper, learning of the dissatisfaction here, had at Professor Whitman's house met and engaged one morning the majority of our staff, his intentions and even his presence being unknown to me. Those to whom we paid $4,000, he gave $7,000; to those we paid $2,000, he offered $4,000, etc., taking even instructors, docents, and fellows. . . .
>
> When this was done he called on me inviting me also to join the hegira at a salary larger than I was receiving—which of course I refused—and then told me what he had done. I replied that it was an act of wreckage for us, comparable to anything that the worst trust had ever attempted against its competitors. . . .

Conversely, some universities—far from venturing out on star raids—fall into the habit of departmental "inbreeding," hiring their own Ph.D.'s. Many of the better schools are afraid that this

43

perpetuates low standards or allows standards to sink by keeping new people out of the department—people who might be a measure of how good or how bad the department really is.

To avoid inbreeding, the very best universities run what could be called farm teams. They send their young Ph.D.'s out to lesser—though not always smaller—universities where they are seasoned for a few years and then brought back up to the big leagues. An unfriendly voice might say the system is just another, more roundabout form of inbreeding, whereby only big league rookies get tryouts.

Here is a description of what is involved in trying to break into inbred English departments:

> The Modern Language Association—like the (un) Holy, (non) Roman, (non) Empire—is somewhat misnamed; it is not Modern, it has little to do with Language, and it is anything but an Association. Actually it's a ramshackle collection of some 19,000 professors [mostly English professors, critics, writers] . . . whose interest in literature is second only to their interest in prestige . . . it is divided into a tiny in-group and a vast out-group. . . . The hard core in-group is composed of distinguished men from the most distinguished institutions who come to drink and gossip [at annual meetings] and openly patronize MLA's employment facilities; very few men at Harvard or Yale secured their appointments by using the facilities. The gates . . . are carefully guarded, but the out-group persists in trying to sidle in. Occasionally one makes it. . . .
>
> At the age of thirty, our hero finds himself trying to support his wife and two kids on the monumental largess of $6,435 per annum.
>
> . . . he treks annually to the MLA conference to try his luck at getting in . . . this in-getting business is filled with anfractuosities. Your credentials may be glittering, but if you haven't gone to the right school and taught at the right places, and if you don't know the right people, your chances are virtually nil.

44

You've got to wear the right clothes and have exactly the right air of worldly wisdom mixed with exactly the right amount of enthusiasm for literature. Moreover, the rules keep changing all the time. At the last convention, for example, the in-keepers came up with a brand-new term—"shopworn." A man is shopworn if he has been employed by too many institutions—like a lady employed by too many men.

The conversation descended to the lower ranks of academic life—the assistants, the graduate students. Ken explained the hard economics of his situation: "I have a half-time teaching assistantship, that's about twelve to thirteen hours for nine months. It works out to something like two courses in the fall and one in the spring. They're elementary courses, and we do all the work, and make up the exams. I get $2,400 a year, $245.06 a month after taxes. That's very good. The math department has money. It, and physics, and maybe chemistry pay the best."

"In English it's $215 and you work up," Richard put in.

I asked Ken about his classes.

"They average about twenty-five students, but they start with thirty-five. I try to cut it down. I'm nasty, I give tough quizzes. Thirty-five test papers is too much. You can't do a decent job of grading them. With twenty-four or twenty-five kids I can get to know them . . . I want to teach."

In return for his teaching, Ken also received free tuition, but Johanna had to work. "We were quite lucky," Ken said, "we inherited quite a bit of furniture from grandmother, but some people have to go to the auctions and things to get theirs."

As Ken began to explain that the math assistants are given no training in teaching, a balding, wide-faced, assistant professor of English named Shugrue sat down and joked, "If they make good marks we let them teach; if they don't do well we send them to Indiana—a bad teacher reads aloud to you, you know, like Act III of King Lear; a good teacher teaches inductively."

Ken, the graduate student who must teach, summed it up:

45

"Our bind is doing right by our studies and doing right by our students."

Shugrue seemed to agree, then added, "We all suffer from the desperate struggle to get in contact with the students. I have fifty students in an eighteenth-century literature course. Only the bold people speak up—not the bright ones, but the ones that want to impress you."

"I prefer hearing a professor lecture than listening to him answer ridiculous questions," somebody at our table offered.

"No," somebody else declared. "You can't really learn from straight lectures."

Shugrue took a middle position: "I know more than you, therefore it's worthwhile for me to talk to you professionally, but sometimes it's good for you to say to me 'You're full of shit.' There has to be contact between student and teacher, and students are afraid to see me. Only the flunking students come around—oh, sometimes the A's do, too, but where are all the B's and C's? I know some teachers won't see anybody, but some sit and wait and nobody comes."

The talk shifted to TV lectures, which everybody claimed were mostly used by the Psychology Department. One of the people at the table told a story about watching a TV lecture taped in 1961 which was so hopelessly out of date as to be meaningless. (It concerned contemporary politics.) "Some of these guys use it as a crutch to get out of teaching and revising their notes. It goes on tape, and they play it and replay it every year."

(People in the liberal arts, the humanities in particular, customarily look on teaching machines and TV lectures as unclean objects. They tend to link these devices to the mechanization of the human spirit, but the values involved are somewhat more difficult to judge. Nobody seems to know what a teacher does, so it is hard to know if a machine can do it better. Nevertheless, there is now a fair amount of research on things like TV teaching, and results show that as far as passing tests is concerned, TV students do about as well as others.

46

(The more difficult the class—the more it becomes a matter of understanding ideas, not just knowing things—the more a flesh-and-blood teacher helps. But for many modest learning jobs there is reason to believe that a teaching machine, which instantaneously corrects the student when he makes an error, is superior to a teacher who may need weeks to grade exams and correct themes.)

The implications of the subject are important, but had to be left unexplored, since Catherine and Richard said it was time to leave for Allen Hall if we wanted to get there by one o'clock, the hour when the girls are supposed to be inside their multistory, double-winged dormitory. In the dark winter night, with the lights from the cars in front of it, Allen Hall loomed tall and institutional.

The girls are very closely regulated at the University of Illinois. On weekday nights the women's dorms are closed at 10:30 P.M. and locked. Friday and Saturday, date nights, the hour is 1:00 A.M., and on Sundays it is 11:00 P.M. All the girls, who are called "women" in the printed University regulations—which make it clear that they are considered girls—must be in by lockup time. A little flexibility in the rules permits coeds to stay out to midnight more often as they get older. All the rules, and the formulas for applying them and for granting exceptions, are meticulously written out in a book called *Code On Undergraduate Student Affairs,* Chapter VII, Section C, paragraphs 3 and 4.

If you are late past lockup time for a total of more than ten minutes during a semester you get in serious hot water and are subject to being brought up before a discipline committee. As the system works out in practice, a coed is much less likely to get into trouble if she stays out all night than if she is fifteen minutes late getting back to her dorm. Since bed checks are not made, the most likely way of attracting attention to yourself is being late and having to get somebody to put your name down on the nightly list when she opens the door to let you in. Nobody knows if you're out overnight unless there is a fire drill. But as

Catherine pointed out, "They always tell beforehand when they're going to have a fire drill and they never have them on weekends."

The men can come home whenever they want. At off-campus parties, part of the fun is to see if the coeds can be lured or lulled into staying after 1:00 A.M. "I've been to many, many parties," one coed told me, "where, after it was 1:00 A.M., the boys would go around and find out which of us were undergraduates and then gloat. They knew we had to sleep somewhere."

That a lot of girls do get in by 1:00 A.M was attested to by the scene at Allen Hall that night.

Catherine showed me into the lounge, a carpeted public room where the men, who may not go upstairs in the building, may sit and visit in the comfortable chairs, settees, and couches provided in the big room. All around us were necking, fondling couples.

"There's nothing they can do," Catherine explained. "There's absolutely no place else for them to go, especially in the winter, absolutely no privacy."

As Catherine talked, I looked. Some of the young people, in twos and fours, sat and chatted, but only three or four feet away were lovers, close to horizontal positions on pieces of furniture that were never designed for their present usage.

"They are breaking the three-foot rule," Catherine said, indicating a prone couple on a settee a few feet from us.

"The what?" I whispered.

"There's a rule that all couples must have at least three feet on the floor when sitting in the lounges." (I later asked Mimsie, the Dean of Women, about this, because in the official publications of University rules I could find no word of it. Mimsie said no such rule existed, or ever had as far as she knew, but that some students unshakably believe it does. She said that she had once seen such a rule posted on a dorm bulletin as a joke. It was, however, an indicator of how many of the students view the administration, which they are truly convinced sits up nights concocting such legalistic absurdities.)

"There's also a rule against wearing raincoats in here," Catherine insisted. "Some of the girls used to come down to the lounge with almost nothing on underneath. You can go all the way under a raincoat."

Subsequently I heard similar tales from other people, but an older person must expect students to try to ruffle his moral feathers; they want to see how quickly you become pompous and indignant.

The raincoat story, I finally decided, was a deliberately disturbing restatement of the widespread demand for more privacy. It hardly seemed to describe most of the University's undergraduates who, when I got to know more of them, struck me in general as restrained, constrained, and incapable of performing— much less enjoying—such acts of flamboyant exhibitionism.

Catherine directed my eyes to the dorm windows, at which I could see girls standing. "They spy in here to see who's doing what with their boyfriends, and they talk and gossip about it all week."

"Why aren't they out with their dates?" I wanted to know. Catherine and I both spoke in whispered mumbles out of respect for the passion around us, although the other non-neckers in the room talked at ordinary conversational volume.

"Some of the peekers'll be down in the lounge next week. Some of the other girls can't get dates. They spy and talk for spite and envy."

As the couple nearest us continued their agonizing, a boy walked over and put his head down so that his face could not have been more than eighteen inches from their joined lips and closed eyes. I supposed that he was a friend and that in some way he was communicating with them, though I couldn't understand how. It looked as though he were a voyeur, but it didn't seem to matter to the couple.

A door in the back of the room opened and five girls entered. Pinned on their sweaters and dresses were little oblong pieces of paper on which were printed in crayon: CLOSER. The closers spread out across the lounge and began drawing the tall floor-to-ceiling drapes. When they had finished, they began to pry loose the cleaving couples, saying, "Five minutes to one."

"Sometimes they just come by and tap you on the shoulder," Catherine said.

"Who are the closers?" I wanted to know.

"Girls in the dorm. Everybody takes turns. You do it about twice a semester."

"What if you don't want to be a closer?"

"Oh, you've got to. You get into a lot of trouble if you refuse."

Obedient to the closers, Catherine and I proceeded to the foyer, where there was a forest of necking couples. They reminded me more of stalagmites than trees, of solid, inert mineral deposits than precarious, self-conscious living things. Couples came rushing from the outer doors into the foyer, found a clear spot on the floor to stand, and clamped their bodies and mouths together.

"There's a rule you're not supposed to lean up against the walls either," Catherine explained. "They caught kids doing it leaning up against the walls. That's why the rule."

"It doesn't seem to be strictly enforced," I observed.

"No, it isn't."

Richard had returned and was waiting in the car outside, so Catherine joined him while I stayed awhile and walked among the couples. They paid no attention to me.

The lights were being flickered by the closers. The foyer reluctantly began to empty. I stood outside and watched the young men leave. Some could hardly walk away; they looked back once more at their girls, who stood by the plateglass doors that the closers were locking. Others stamped away, blocked and angry. Some showed no emotion in walk or expression, others were glistening-eyed.

For a moment the flat cement in front of Allen was vacant.

The closers were still behind the glass doors, several with pieces of paper and pencil in hand to take down the names of late-comers. One latecomer, a tall girl, gave her shorter escort a quick, full smack on the lips and then ran to the door. The closers unlocked it, but in keeping with the spirit of the routine, only opened the door about a quarter of the way, so that the tall girl had to slip inside sideways. She was laughing and so were the closers. I didn't see them write down her name. Maybe they gave her a break, but Catherine told me later that if the closers were caught at it they got the same punishment as the latecomer.

We drove off to another part of town, going up and down sloping streets for a long while until we reached a small cottage on the crest of a hill. A party was going on in the living room, which obviously had been dirty before the party started.

"Don't say who you are," Catherine warned me, "or they won't say anything to you."

"They" crowded the small living room, lined the walls, and sat on dilapidated couches. The music was rock 'n' roll again, and the people were wearing very tight jeans and cuffless trousers, and the girls wore boots.

It was too noisy to carry on a conversation. Nobody tried. Some danced, or sat on the couches and chairs like bus riders, looking straight ahead; others stood and drank without words. People came up to me, not so much to talk, but to shout explanatory information into my ear. Nobody asked who or what I was. Perhaps they knew. In any case they seemed to think I was someone who should be told things.

A face and a shouting voice: "Don's here. Did you see Don?"

A second face and shouting voice: "You know who Don is? Don's the one they arrested for narcotics."

First face and shouting voice: "He's been up in Chicago since it happened. Ya want to talk to Don? He could tell you a lot. There's a lot of marijuana on this campus."

Second face and shouting voice: "Like hell there is."

51

The face of a weeping, snuffling blond girl passed into the kitchen: "Oh God, where's Henry? God, where is he? I've got his cigarette. I've got his Lucky Strike."

A third face and shouting voice: "A lot of these girls are undergraduate women. [I was struck by his use of the official administration expression.] They shouldn't be here. They'll have to stay out all night. Some of the undergraduate men have apartments they're not supposed to have—some of the girls'll stay there."

I leaned over and shouted into the third face's ear, "Where will the other girls stay?"

"Some'll stay with girl friends. Some'll stay with graduate students who're allowed to have off-campus apartments. It doesn't have to mean the girl's going to do something if she stays at a man's apartment. Some of them may just stay here. This party probably won't break up till breakfast."

A fourth face and shouting voice: "They don't fight much at these parties. This's the Slob Contingent, they look rough but they aren't. Sometimes there's trouble when people from the fraternities or the engineering schools or something crash in, but this is liberal arts, and they're peaceful."

I found Catherine sitting like a public transit rider on one of the couches. She introduced me to the person she was sitting next to, but I told her I was tired and hungry and wanted to leave. She said she did, too.

Outside it had turned colder, and big snowflakes were shooting down from invisible night clouds. Catherine and I made our way through several backyards to an all-night gas station, where we called a cab to take us to a restaurant.

While eating, Catherine complained about the crowd at the party. "They don't do anything. They're critical, they have brains, but they're on the outskirts of the University. They get good people, people who could do something and soon they're drinking too much, spending their time not doing anything. They're degenerates. Sometimes people break away from them,

52

and go back to school and start studying again or maybe go to another university."

"Doesn't every university always have a group of hangers-on," I countered, "the undecided, the cynical, and the vicious?"

"No, this is our generation."

I couldn't help but wonder why every collegiate group has to think of itself as set apart by history. "What is a generation, anyhow?" I asked myself, too tired to voice the question. I was angry because I had expected—although I hadn't been promised it—a party with real talk, and instead I had gotten a party of dancing fools who needed alcohol before their sex. Catherine was telling me it was all a special spirit infused into their generation. I wanted to tell her that people had been drinking to stupefaction and then making love for thousands of years. Instead I asked, "In a hundred years will anybody think that you and I weren't part of the same generation? After all what's fifteen or twenty years? We think the people born in 1830 and 1850 were born more or less at the same time."

"We're the first atomic generation. The first to grow up knowing that at any time the world can be destroyed."

"Mine actually saw it used."

"That's it. Yours saw it used. Our generation has the bomb, but it doesn't know what it is like. Most of us were still in grammar school when the Korean War ended."

"So?"

"We're worried and we're selfish."

The conversation drifted off toward love and sex. She had lived with a man for a while when she was out of school. She said she knew a lot about men. Maybe she did, but it was almost dawn and I was too tired to continue the conversation.

After dropping Catherine at her house, I leaned back in the cab and looked out at the empty Champaign business streets where here and there a storekeeper had neglected to turn off an electric Santa Claus. The big snowflakes were still throwing themselves out of the sky and melting instantly on the macadam, tar black in contrast to the white spots coming down on it.

53

4

The Problems Aren't New

A bamboo screen had been hung in the vast oblong living room of the McKinley Foundation, the Presbyterian student center, concealing the great Norman fireplace. If you kept your eyes on the screen which came down almost to the green rug, you might forget the room had brick walls and devolved out of a tradition brought to England a thousand years ago by that Gallicized Viking, William the Conqueror.

In the room on this particular Sunday there was the son of a tradition several thousand years older. A young man of grace and beauty, he wore a superbly cut black silk robe and sandals; the forceful grace with which he performed every movement was so commanding that the incongruity of his sprinkling incense on a General Electric hot plate passed unnoticed.

Seated on settees and chairs in a semicircle before the bamboo screen were about fifteen of William the Conqueror's descendants. These Anglo-Normans, translated by time and geography into members of the University community at Champaign, Illinois, were in sharp contrast to Shozo Sato as he laid out the firepot and the other equipment used in the Japanese tea ceremony. They were attentive, respectful, even reverential, as the young man of Japan made ready to initiate them into his civilization.

They were trying hard to show they were appreciative and grateful but betrayed a certain nervousness.

"If you would care to," Shozo Sato said softly, indicating by a broad yet restrained gesture of the arm that he meant that the Anglo-Normans should sit on the floor near him. His heavy silk robe imparted a definiteness to his figure as he sat erect, his legs under his body. "In Japan," he explained, "we sit this way," and his flat hand, palm upward, fingers pointed toward himself, outlined the line of his posture. He looked at the willing but clumsy Anglo-Norman males getting out of the deeply upholstered couches, and a grazing look of distress crossed the features of his broadly handsome, Asian face.

Two of the women managed to sit in the proper Japanese way, but the men floundered. Shozo Sato tried another approach: "Perhaps you would be more comfortable in this position?" and he quickly assumed the American manner of sitting on a floor. "It is customary for us to have the tea ceremony without wearing shoes," he went on and then added with a hopeful tone in his voice, "You may find it comfortable—restful." Most of the men took off their shoes.

"The tea ceremony is supposed to be very quiet, restful for the soul. Now we will bow. This is the sign of the beginning of the tea ceremony," he said in a light tone, bowing deeply, easily, and without strain. The Anglo-Normans bowed too. Some put their most reverential faces on, the look that says, "We are in the presence of knowledge and we are learning." Others had looks of piety on their faces, but who knows on what gods and spirits they were meditating.

Shozo Sato began the stylized ritual of the tea ceremony in a silence that made highly audible the small noise of water-dripping ceramics gently touching each other. He took a ladle of water from the bronze firepot, explaining, "We enjoy the sound of water boiling." Next he drifted into a thoughtful soliloquy while he ceremonially washed the tea equipment and heated heavy, foaming tea. It was stridently green, far greener and

55

richer than the weak pastel greens in the Japanese pictures hanging in the Illini Union exhibition.

"In your mind when you do this, you are not cleaning bamboo, you are cleaning yourself. Children are born, old people die, the tea bowl breaks, it is gone like the people when they die. . . . What is left? A famous name, a work of art, a bad name? The tea ceremony is like Zen philosophy, which keeps asking Why? Who am I? Why . . . why?"

The Anglo-Normans tried to keep very still, but several of them surreptitiously wiggled their stockinged toes.

Later, a short, frail girl with dark hair and very white skin tinted with delicious apple-red came into Larry Hill's office. Larry told me that she, like big Wally, had been a civil rights worker in Mississippi during the past summer. Her emotional anxiety was evident when she asked Larry if there could be a chapel service that night. It was only a couple of days after the FBI had arrested a score of Mississippi men for the murder of three youthful civil rights workers; later they were released by a Mississippi United States Commissioner. "I need somebody to say something about Mississippi," she said. "I need to have this explained. I'm about ready to shout at Ida; I can hardly look at her. [Ida was a white Presbyterian girl from Mississippi, studying at the University.] I think chapel would help."

Cautiously and kindly, Larry asked, "Well, what did you have in mind?"

"Just something simple. To pray over it and somebody to say a few words. I think I really need it, and so do some of the others."

"We'll work out something," Larry answered.

When the girl left, Larry explained that the situation was difficult. Ida, unbelievably, had been dating Wally; her parents had been understanding enough to begin a tentative correspondence with him. What they didn't know was that Wally had taken Ida to a Negro fraternity dance where she had actually danced with Negro boys. The relationship had been shattering for everybody, and it had been going on since the beginning of the semester.

Today's student political activity is a rephrasing of an old question. It was the slavery issue which first pitted students against college authorities on a political question. During the Revolutionary War, students dressed like Indians and joined their fathers in destroying British-taxed tea; but prior to the 1830's most student rebellions had been about things like food and discipline. Slavery changed that. J. H. Fairchild, who was both a student at and president of Oberlin College, the first college to admit Negroes and women—in that order—recalled what happened at Lane Seminary near Cincinnati when the students there were carried away by the opinions of the abolitionist agitator William Lloyd Garrison:

> The students requested of the Faculty the use of the public room occupied as a chapel, for the discussion of slavery. The Faculty recommended quiet—rather discountenanced discussion, but did not prohibit it. The students gathered in the chapel, and for eighteen successive evenings continued their debate. At the outset there was great diversity of sentiment, but in the end the antislavery view prevailed unanimously.
>
> . . . Movements like these disturbed the quiet of the Trustees of the Seminary, some of whom were wholly men of commerce, and understood better the pork market than the management of a literary institution. Others sympathized in the general apprehension of evil from the antislavery excitement.
>
> The Summer vacation . . . came on. . . . The Trustees held a meeting at this juncture, and passed a law . . . prohibiting the discussion of slavery among the students, both in public and in private. They were not to be allowed to communicate with each other on the subject, even at the table in the Seminary commons. . . . The students returned to enter their protest

57

against the oppressive gag-law of the Trustees, and to ask dismissions from the institution. Four-fifths of them left in a body, and Lane Seminary has to this day scarce recovered from the blow. . . .

The interesting thing about the student abolitionist rows was they seemed to be intracollegiate affairs more than the massing of students against the practice of slavery itself. Since transportation and communication is easier today, there is a good deal of contact between students in different universities, and the grouping of large numbers of students to go into the South, say, and strike a blow directly, is more easily done.

The next epoch of student action was considerably less violent. Starting in the late 1880's (coeval with the ballooning of the reforming progressivism of William Jennings Bryan and Teddy Roosevelt), college students went into the big city slums to found and to work in settlement houses. Students from Chicago, Harvard, Northwestern, Vassar, Wisconsin, and other colleges, gave time and energy to provide education and missionary uplift to Catholic and Jewish immigrants in what might be called "Domestic Peace Corps #1."

Student political activity on any big scale then disappeared until the Depression and the 1930's, when it assumed a form and a tone surprisingly similar to that of white northern college student activity in Mississippi and Berkeley during the past few years.

In 1932, the coal miners and the coal mineowners of Harlan County, Kentucky were accustomed to settle their labor disputes by shot and shell, but in the new Depression, students developed an interest in and a sympathy for the miners and their blood struggles. In March, 1932, students from Harvard, Smith, and Columbia chartered a bus to "bloody Harlan" for what they described as an investigatory mission, but which the folks on the mineowners' side in Kentucky considered outside agitating. You wouldn't have to change many names in this account of what happened then in Kentucky to have a 1960 description of a student freedom-ride in Alabama.

And at Cumberland Gap, the mountain pass into Kentucky, the full impact of Kentucky law and order descended. The road was almost dark when the bus turned the corner over the boundary; out of the approaching night the scowling faces of a mob of more than 200 people greeted the visitors. Cars drove up and surrounded the bus; most of the throng were armed, wearing the badges of deputy sheriffs. . . . When a student sought to address the crowd to explain the peaceful purpose of the delegation, he found that his auditors had been incited too intensely . . . to heed any reason. There were derisive catcalls, then the ominous lynch cry: "String 'em up."

At this point District Attorney Smith delivered a speech which inflamed the mob further and dramatically revealed the mentality of a ranking official of Kentucky. He announced that the students were "Yankees, aliens and agitators," then reversed himself and proclaimed that they were not students at all but revolutionists in disguise.

A month later the editor of the Columbia University *Spectator,* the student newspaper, was expelled for criticizing about everything from student discipline to the dining halls. "Student indignation crystallized . . . when a mass meeting was held on the Library Steps with more than 4,000 students present. Columbia had never witnessed . . . so impressive an outpouring of serious and determined students. And there, a University strike of major proportions was voted. . . ."

Conservative student groups also made their presence known by tossing eggs at the protestors and calling them communists. But if a few hundred followed conservative leadership, "close to seventy-five percent of the 1,800 students in the college, augmented by hundreds from other schools of the University went on strike." As at Berkeley, the University had to back down, and also, as at Berkeley, it seemed that political action by students off campus flowed back onto it as the rebels used their newly learned agitational techniques against their own administration.

After dinner, Larry and I headed for the Turkshead coffee house on Green Street. The inside was attractive in a sort of traditional coffee-house fashion. The usual little tables stood on a floor of big black-and-white squares, and the light in the room was warm, but dim, dark red.

Larry and I had been there only a short time when we were joined by Bill Hirt, a tall senior who sported a moustache and came from a Chicago suburb. We also acquired a short, highly energetic full professor of civil engineering.

Bill's tone was disillusioned. "I'll be graduated in June and I won't feel more educated then than I do now. What I'll have then is an arbitrary piece of paper."

"You'll need it," the professor said, his dark, intelligent eyes taking Bill's measure. "You need it to get your Ph.D., and the Ph.D. is *the* union card."

"That's just it," Bill interrupted.

"What's wrong with that?" the professor asked. "Unions can be abused, but they keep up standards, too, you know."

I asked them about the quality of the teaching at the University, and whether the pressure to do research gets in the way. Bill's observation was mournful: "I can name you people who just use this institution and yet they're in teaching situations. There are some good teachers but you don't see them much."

The professor disagreed. "I don't think you'll really find many poor teachers. Most teachers are available to their students."

Young Bill and the professor, arguing about what college teachers *should* do and *should* be like, were talking about two different, long-recognized types in higher education. Sociologists call them "locals" and "cosmopolitans." Bill was for the locals, and the professor liked the cosmopolitans, probably because he was one.

The mark of the local is the teacher with strong loyalty to the college or university where he works. He is willing to help build up the institution; often he will be a well-known figure in the college town, someone personally known to the civic organizations, and perhaps, if he is working for a state school, to the legislators. A local is more apt to be known as a good teacher than a cosmopolitan, not because he necessarily is, but because he is more inclined to help with student activities, social affairs, and clubs; he therefore has a better chance of making a campus reputation. Locals seldom enjoy much repute as scholars; usually nobody outside of their institutions has ever heard of them.

Cosmopolitans are the reverse. The people whose good opinion the professor courts are his fellow professionals in schools like Massachusetts Institute of Technology, Cal Tech, or Illinois Institute of Technology.

The cosmopolitan does "use" the school, for to the cosmopolitan the school is merely the place where he can do his work and build his professional reputation. Although there is no convincing evidence to show that cosmopolitans are worse teachers than locals, there is a good deal to indicate their most enthusiastic student-admirers are would-be cosmopolitans, future specialists in the same disciplines. Just as they are less interested in the other students, so the other students are less interested in them; hence their not-always-merited reputation for indifference.

The cosmopolitans are the academic nomads; it is they who must really publish or perish (that is, stay put on the faculty of some minor league university); they are the ones who are always pushing for "higher standards," for more research, for bigger graduate school programs. The cosmopolitans with access to government research money and the foundations have the whip hand, since it is the cosmopolitans who have become the symbols of "excellence"; they are the ones who offer the hope of getting an American to the moon ahead of the Russians. In the mature stages of their careers, the cosmopolitans may become the "captains of research," generals of the research armies, professors who teach not and neither do they publish.

In many institutions there is a certain tension between the two types, despite their needing each other. There are exceptions, of course, as at Harvard, where because there is no higher place to climb, you can be both a local and a cosmopolitan at the same time. Other exceptions would be the weaker denominational schools, the junior or community colleges, or the downtown night school type of college—in such places there are usually too few cosmopolitans to cause much of a fuss. It is at the in-between places where you can see the tension at work.

David Riesman's account of the situation he observed at the University of Buffalo's Law School is instructive:

At least half the faculty and all but one of its younger men were Harvard trained, for at that time Harvard dominated legal education, the world of the nationally oriented law schools, as no university now dominates legal, medical, or graduate education. Most of these Harvard-trained people wanted to teach those courses which, as students, they had learned were the subjects of greatest prestige. . . . As against this, several of us thought we should develop a curriculum that was not merely a minor league version of the Eastern Seaboard schools but rather one which was designed with reference to the particular problems of Western New York. But such a change . . . would have been defined as an intellectual defeat, as having become provincial under the impact of local pressures, as a discredited vocationalism concerned with the State bar exams and the local job market. Thus the experiment was never made (I might add . . . that all my Harvard-trained colleagues, except for the Dean, are now back at Harvard) . . . as it turned out the good students were in only a few cases interested in preparing themselves for careers confined to Upper

New York State; for most of them, their models were their itinerant [cosmopolitan] teachers, and their eyes were on what the Supreme Court was up to . . . and not on Buffalo's City Planning Commission. . . . In contrast, the home guard faculty [the locals] had on the whole little to offer . . . they were apt to recall how it had been in their day, but failed to see . . . in what ways an institution has to change in order to remain the same."

Whatever the cosmopolitans' achievements, they must also take much of the blame for present practices in the system of academic promotion. Not that cosmopolitans are particularly defensive about the publish-or-perish policy or the mountains of unread dissertations in the world's libraries. The professor in the coffee house, for example, complained not about the system, but its ponderousness: "We always realize that much of what is published is merely acceptable, not great. A man is being asked to publish a few trivial things and then he can go back to his great work, if he's doing any. We also realize that not all journals are the same. Academic journals come in two categories, referral and nonreferral.

"A referral journal is one that sends your article out to three or four men in the field before it's accepted; a nonreferral journal has its articles accepted by the editors alone. Today many deans don't count articles in nonreferral journals for promotion . . . the trouble is, though, that by the time three or four men approve your article for a referral journal it may take a year."

There are other ways of scoring promotion points. Instead of writing an article in a journal, you can take over the editorship or, failing that, you can start your own journal. Another way is to edit books of other peoples' articles. The modern publishing professor also knows how to make good use of his graduate students. Men who have rarely put pen to paper have made reputations for themselves by cultivating this new skill of administrative authorship. (Professors also have been known to make money, if not prestige, by using their positions to make graduate students do unpaid, free work for them on outside moonlighting research and consulting jobs. Professional moonlighting is a common practice condoned by schools that allow it rather than pay higher salaries, but it raises ethical questions seldom talked about outside of graduate student circles.)

In actuality, most college teachers never publish. They work in schools away from the academic big time where one nonpublishing teacher would only have to be replaced by another. For the most part, the publishing pressure is confined to universities like Illinois with big graduate schools. One study showed that the top universities with less than ten percent of the faculty in higher education cranked out almost forty percent of the articles in the learned journals. Even the big universities do not get rid of all the nonpublishers, although the case of Charles T. "Copey" Copeland, adored by generations of Harvard undergraduates, demonstrates the difficulty of advancement in such a situation. Made an instructor in English in 1892, he taught (and did not publish) for nearly twenty years before being promoted to an assistant professorship. Copey's career makes it clear that publish-or-perish antedates the postwar era, computers, "bigness," and other current complaints. It was built into the American university as the latter was being formed at the end of the nineteenth century, and because it is so close to a university's operating definition of itself, the practice will not be abandoned merely because some people condemn it. The universities of today hold to the 1894 position of William Rainey Harper, the president of the University of Chicago: "The University . . . will be patient, but it expects from every man honest and persistent effort in the direction of contribution to the world's knowledge."

By the 1940's—more than a generation ago—publish-or-perish was a common complaint and an accepted necessity:

The meaning of research is so equivocal that almost any sort of investigative enterprise may be connoted, but academic

64

men ordinarily have in mind the kind of inquiry that yields publishable results.

. . . intellectual inquiry, unlike the growing of mushrooms, is not carried on in hidden recesses away from the public gaze. There is the necessity for bringing results to light in the form of publication, for in the academic scheme of things results unpublished are little better than those never achieved. . . . Situational imperatives dictate a "publish or perish" credo. . . .

In 1958, almost sixty years after Daniel Coit Gilman had said academic publishing was getting out of hand, his judgment was restated with bitter emphasis in a book that caused a lot of talk but no change in the system. Its authors quote a professor whose colleague has been refused promotion because he spent too much time with a group and not enough on research:

". . . it was clear that his really tremendous work with this student group hadn't been weighted at all in the consideration of his promotion. He did a really tremendous job. It caused the rest of us to decide that if this kind of activity was not what was honored—and he'd led them to several national recognitions—then we'd do what was honored—namely, sitting in the library and writing weighty papers, and let their goddamned student group go to hell, which it has."

Neither Bill nor Larry nor the professor evidenced much familiarity with the history of publish-or-perish or any of the other institutional problems that agitated them. They drank their coffee, propounded their points at each other, and talked as though the university had been created *de novo* the year before last. It was like listening to three men who are ignorant of American history before 1945 talk about the growth of federal power; their facts may be correct but they have no guide for arranging them. Without history to moderate their judgments, their conversation was tonelessly abstract; without reference to specific men and events, their reasoning was entirely founded on undemonstrable

65

first principles of man. The same tonelessness runs through a lot of contemporary criticism of higher education, as if going to a school or teaching in one can charter you as an authority. Not that this hampers coffee-house debate. That at the Turkshead ran past closing time.

The Passing of Chief Illiniwek

It was cold out. Students walked the Euclidian lines of the quadrangle to breakfast and early-morning classes. In front of the Union, on Green Street—the main east-west street which runs between Champaign and Urbana—the green Illibuses stopped to load and unload students. The campus is so big that without them nobody would be on time.

Immediately west of the Georgian Union building is a stone Romanesque classroom building, Altgeld Hall, which honors the only Illinois politician, aside from Lincoln, who may have a valid claim to greatness. I stopped a coed to ask who it was that this towered building of rough-cut stone was named after.

"He was a botany professor, I think. I'm not sure. He was very famous once, but he died a long time ago," she said prettily. "I think they'd be able to tell you in the Union."

Is Altgeld, the great governor whom Vachel Lindsay called "Eagle Forgotten," part of the living tradition here or only subject matter for the English and history departments? Every freshman is given a thickish, attractive booklet called *Illini Guidelines*. I wondered what the book might say about Altgeld; a university was, after all, once upon a time, the storehouse of the acts and thoughts of men who have come before us. On page six, there is a paragraph entitled "TRADITIONS." It says: "Students come and go, but traditions grow and usually remain, weaving a thread of continuity between one generation of students and the next. The University of Illinois, now drawing near its hundredth birthday, can count on many traditions."

Elsewhere in the book I did find mention of "The Altgeld Chimes in the tower of Altgeld Hall. . . . The chimes were the gift of the classes of 1910 through 1920."

How is a university with more than 25,000 students occupied with everything from "Boolean Algebras with Applications to Computer Circuits" (Math 391) to "Le Théâtre Français depuis 1800" (French 317) and "Bacteriological Control of Dairy Plants" (Food Science 211) to have a tradition? The University has students from every county in Illinois, every state in the Union, and, it would seem, every nation on the globe. How are people of such indescribable diversity to receive, enrich, and bequeath any single tradition, unless it be a synthetic one like Chief Illiniwek, who was invented in 1926 to parade around football games in a feathered regalia?

This is a university without ivy, literally and figuratively. Most of the buildings are bare of it, and the newer glass-and-cement structures couldn't support the plant. I was told that back in 1920, when there were only about 7,000 students on the campus, the University seemed to be trying to develop traditions comparable to those of the prestige eastern schools. But the multiversity, to use that ugly but perhaps descriptive word, is not the leisured, timeless haven of the sons and daughters of the well-to-do who are being "cultivated" so that the scepter of government and rulership may in due time be given them. It is where the thousands, the ten thousands, come to be trained, and what this has done is nicely, although inadvertently, described in one paragraph in *Illini Guidelines*, also in the section called "LANDMARKS": "The Senior Bench, gift of the class of 1900, is located between Altgeld Hall and the Illini Union. Some years ago, the bench actually was reserved for seniors; this custom has vanished

68

and the bench is available for anyone who chooses to use it."

Chief Illiniwek, the Columbia lion, and the Wisconsin badger are the hand-me-downs from the great time of the American college when the institution's purposes were only vaguely and occasionally educational. Writing in 1912, Alexander Meiklejohn of the University of Wisconsin, a man who played a prominent part in the battle to make the college a place of learning, could say:

> In a hundred different ways the friends of the college, students, trustees, and even colleagues, seemed to . . . misunderstand its mission . . . to minimize or to falsify its intellectual ideals. The college is a good place for making friends; it gives excellent experience in getting on with men; it has exceptional advantages as an athletic club; it is a relatively safe place for a boy when he first leaves home; on the whole it may improve a student's manners; it gives acquaintance with lofty ideas of character, preaches the doctrine of social service, exalts the virtues and duties of citizenship.

The thought that college, in addition to being a school, was also a place for character building and good morals is an old one among American educators. Princeton's president John Witherspoon used this argument back in 1772 in hopes of getting parents to send their sons to Princeton instead of to England: "The second reason for preferring an American education is that their [the students'] morals may be more effectually preserved. . . . The danger they run of contracting vicious habits by being sent to Britain has been often complained of. . . . There are also in every considerable place in Great Britain, but especially the principal cities where the Colleges are fixed, a constant succession and variety of intoxicating diversions such as Balls, Concerts, Plays, Races, and others. These . . . are highly pernicious to youth in the first stages of their education. . . ."

The subsequent development of our colleges was highly favorable to intoxicating diversions; it was education that was having a hard time surviving in the student-dominated, tradition-ridden, fun-loving school. Here is a description of Yale as it was run in the age of its great football coach, Walter Camp, he of the first All-Americans:

The undergraduates were paying more and more attention to extracurricular activities . . . some literary, some musical or social, some chiefly managerial, some of a money-making sort. All were voluntary. In none did a student have to participate. But most were thoroughly organized, time consuming, highly competitive. . . . Every Freshman was urged to "go out" for something. And no man with social ambitions—unless he were already an athlete or unusually well connected—ignored this extracurriculum, this second race course. . . .

Athletics also made heroes for the underclassmen, excitement for the whole College, spectacles for the world. The annual contests against Harvard and Princeton had become epic battles, anticipated with anxiety, watched almost with agony, and celebrated as befitted Homeric victories.

In addition to athletics and extracurricular activities, Yale College boasted a society system which, in its Senior Societies of Skull and Bones (est. 1832), Scroll and Key (1842), and Wolf's Head (1883), came close to dominating undergraduate life.

In the years immediately before and after World War I, some college educators resolved not to take ignorance lying down and began various programs to attempt to teach their charges more than the barest of minimums. Frank Aydelotte, president of Swarthmore, who instituted one of the earliest and most influential of such programs, was not against the extracurriculum but believed in some kind of intellectual stature. But when Aydelotte began his work at Swarthmore, a small, wealthy, Quaker college near Philadelphia, the college learned that breaking "the academic lock step" of mediocrity would change the whole substance of student life, the whole extracurriculum.

The college that bred fraternity domination, football as a public pageant, and so much that the old grads of the twenties and thirties lovingly remember was also the college that was spiked with anti-intellectuality, with scorn for books as somewhat less than manly, and with a conviction that good students were "grinds" and "wonks." The old student culture of collegiate tradition was inimical to the new campus dominated by undergraduate intellectuals.

When Aydelotte started at Swarthmore, he does not appear to have intended to scrap the old culture. He abolished athletic scholarships, but not football. Nonetheless, just a few years after the new academic program had been put into effect, women's fraternities (the Swarthmorism for sorority) were being attacked by the students and with some doubts the administration finally acquiesced in the students abolishing them.

The senior honorary society was next to be dismantled by the new noncollegiate collegians. A Swarthmore dean has explained what happened: "In the spring on Thursday nights the Book and Key members would rise early from dinner and march in solemn silence to their weekly meeting. Their departure from the dining room was regarded as a traditional ceremony to be gazed upon with respect and awe. It was indeed a revolution in campus attitudes that later produced boos and laughter and even resulted occasionally in barricaded dining room doors."

Dean Hunt remarks that Aydelotte "never succeeded in making social conservatives out of his intellectual radicals." Robert M. Hutchins at the University of Chicago was to learn the same thing a few years later. But the students' social radicalism was not confined to antifraternityism, which is something many egalitarian Americans can sympathize with. By 1930, the Swarthmorians were attacking rules for proper dress. Dean Hunt explains the administration tried its best to keep the boys in shirts with ties and the girls in skirts, but it was a losing battle: "When I left the Dean's Office it was still the custom to exclude barefoot students from the dining room, and this in the spring was becoming something of an increasing problem. The natural love of casting off shoes and stockings and cavorting barefoot upon the green was spreading widely. . . ."

The incoming intellectual student culture did not take over from the Winsockie culture without incident:

> Shortly after the war, when feeling between veterans and nonveterans was as much a complication as fraternity membership, four athletic veterans belonging to the same fraternity took a nonathletic, nonfraternity beard grower to their fraternity house and told him to shave "or else." He shaved. This roused great indignation in some quarters and gratified amusement in others. Another nonathletic, nonfraternity individualist immediately announced that he would grow a mustache, and publicly and repeatedly dared any person or persons to interfere. Shorty before graduation day, the same four veterans visited this boy in his room at night and with clippers cut two perpendicular swaths in his hair. One of the liberal student organizations drafted a document . . . in which they asserted the rights of every individual to grow hair as he pleased and demanded that the faculty punish any persons who attempted to violate this right.

The Dean concludes by saying that "with the increasing popularity of beards and the declining feeling among fraternity members that they can successfully interfere with nonconformists, this particular issue has faded . . ." but the incident tells much about the old and the new campus ways. The old way was the way of the group, of inarticulate anger when the group's method of living was violated; it was the way of "school spirit." The new intellectuals abominate "school spirit"; they are far more articulate, everything is a matter of principle, and, when crossed, they will shout the house down.

The difference in the two styles is never clearer than in their respective approaches to sex. The fraternity boy was supposed to have been wildly promiscuous. Whether he really was or not, it is certainly true that when he was caught breaking college rules on the subject he "took his medicine," as they used to say back in the days when Frank Merriwell went to Yale. The new intellectual does not. He argues right or necessity, has managed to loosen many regulations, and in the process has won himself a reputation as a hedonist, as well as a beatnik and a red. Dean Hunt quotes Swarthmore's student newspaper, the *Phoenix,* in a 1948 editorial written after the publication of the Kinsey report on American male sexual practices:

> Our first response to reading the Kinsey report was to write a blasting editorial . . . and to call on the administration to face the realities of the situation by finding more adequate facilities on the campus for sexual expression by the student body.
>
> The Kinsey report showed also that the amount of sexual activity on the part of the college male is far in excess of that recognized by the institution of college, the total sexual outlet for the typical single white male in the top educational category between the ages of 16 and 25 being approximately two orgasms a week.
>
> . . . It is evident that the liberalization of administrative policy on sexual affairs can only be achieved *sub rosa,* without the publicity attendant upon open avowal.

As might be expected, the alumni were aroused, the *Phoenix* was suspended for a few weeks, and the *Harvard Crimson,* long since captured by the new student intelligentsia, charged a violation of academic freedom. Nonetheless the episode nicely illustrates the new and old styles, and points up one reason that everybody can sit on the Senior Bench at Champaign.

Swarthmore is one of perhaps twenty colleges and universities that set styles and show the way. At Swarthmore, the last rah-rah has been uttered; these are still to be heard at most American schools. At Illinois, only several years ago, a faculty member was discharged for writing a letter to the *Daily Illini* that was a good deal less provocative than what the *Phoenix* had said about sex a decade before. Moreover, a college like Swarthmore gets just about the best of the high school crop, the kids who are able to do much more than score good grades. While Illinois gets good students, even a fair number that would excel at a place like Swarthmore, its undergraduates, by and large, do not come from homes and schools that nurture daring intellectuality and high culture. Thus, Illinois seems a blend of old and new, of tradition and no tradition.

If the University does have a tradition, it may be contained in its noncommittally general motto: "Learning and Labor." What you should learn or labor at is not stated; it is enough to tell the students in effect, "Work!" The learning-and-labor idea is executed in marble and metal in front of Altgeld Hall in the shape of a very large three-figured statue by Lorado Taft, an alumnus. The work has none of the liquidness, none of the melodically curving shapes of most of Taft's work, of which some fine examples can be found on the campus. Instead the blacksmith (labor) and the Minerva (learning) and the motherly Alma Mater are done in the heavy pomposity of the third revival of Greco-Roman style.

Michelle, the art student whom I'd met my first night on campus, had invited me to watch a Hall Board Meeting at Van Doren, a girl's dorm. The Hall Board consists of students from each floor in the dorm; it functions, within narrow limits, as a unit of self-government and the means by which the larger University hopes to touch individual lives.

Although it was barely five when we arrived, there were several kissing stalagmites in the Van Doren lounge as we went through to a basement room where the meeting was going to be held. The Hall Board president, a dark-haired, ardent sociology major, was already present, and in the next few minutes, about ten more young women came into the room, some in lipstick and rather dressy clothes, others in jeans and sweaters. The majority didn't

74

wear makeup; this was true of many girls on campus, particularly if they had reasonably good complexions.

When they were all assembled, a fine-arts education student with a witty way and an animated face rolled her eyes and, gesturing with a thumb past a closed door, drawled out, "Shall I get her?" "Her" was the house mother. They said "Yes," and the girl, Naomi, went out and came back with a middle-aged woman who walked with her eyes down, sat behind the girls during the meeting, and kept silent throughout except once when she spoke up to say of some suggestion, "You can't do that. You don't have the power to."

The president opened the meeting by saying, "A lot of people have complained that they put up beige drapes on all the windows and have taken away all the shades. (Significantly, the students seldom refer to themselves as "kids," and "they" is usually the administration or some other unseen, hostile, irrational power.)

"One of the deans will be here tonight to explain why. Anybody who's got any questions can ask them tonight, so will you tell everybody?"

The president quickly guided the meeting to the real order of business. "People have been coming up to me and complaining. Some come and say, we're independents, non-sorority people; why are you pushing us into activities and meetings? They say things like 'Leave us alone and stop trying to get us to go on hayrides.' Then others are saying, 'We're an organized dorm, why don't we do more?'"

This produced an immediate response: "The people on my floor are so angry at being called out for dorm meetings once a week that they don't listen and they won't participate."

Another girl: "The problem is, are we going to have any activities at all? We work and push to set up an activity, then only twenty-five or thirty people show up."

"Maybe we could have some voluntary activities," Michelle drawled, "like, you know, put aside one table for faculty dinners

75

for a dean or professors, but before you invited somebody you'd better be sure there'd be eight people anyway. . . ."

"Well, then that's compulsory too. I mean it's not spontaneous," somebody objected in the mild manner of talking these girls had.

"Nothing's spontaneous," another girl replied. "I mean you have to plan, if you're going to do anything."

The president wanted a decision: "What's the Hall Board's reaction? To have nothing compulsory?"

A blond girl didn't like that idea: "In a way we have a moral purpose with the University to help make people well rounded. We have to have activities."

The debate became general with contributions from all sides:

—"The hayride failed because of lack of communication. You're giving in to people who don't want to do anything."

—"We don't have enthusiasm, that's our trouble."

—"There're so many things going on already, why does the dorm have to push too?"

—"Nobody takes advantage of activities when we have them."

—"Look at the Christmas tree-trimming party. It was a success."

—"That's because there was free food."

—"Well, there was free food at the hayride."

—"The hayride was dating. Some girls don't want to date."

—"People just don't want to be active. At homecoming I had to go through the corridors saying we need people to decorate."

—"You've got to publicize. When they have Beethoven they don't just say here it is, 16,000 seats. They publicize. That's part of the enthusiasm of the university."

"Anything only so long as we don't have to go through the dorms saying, 'We need you, we need you.' Let's only have meetings when we need to have a meeting, and then it should be compulsory."

The discussion ended without a decision. I had the impression they had talked about the topic before and would again.

The meeting was an example of the old and new collegiate

styles contending with each other. The old style was organizational, for school spirit, for finding out what is expected of them by custom; the new style is irreverent, mildly anarchistic, anti-rah-rah—estranged from institutional, and even group, loyalties. The girls' dorms like this one were perhaps passing through a transition, and some of the unsureness the girls displayed may have been due to their not yet having found a positive meaning in the new dispensation.

We left the meeting, and after an unappetizing but "balanced" meal in the cheerless cafeteria, went back to the lounge at Van Doren. The kissing stalagmites were still kissing, but soon ten or fifteen girls were floating in and out of the conversation. The topics floated, too, as we talked about high schools:

—"Over half of my high school class is here."

—"I go blocks out of my way to avoid my only high school classmate."

—"Suburban high schools put more emphasis on working than do Chicago high schools."

—"Another difference is that in Chicago we had a bunch of old bags for teachers."

There was talk about being Jewish or Negro, about the town and the townspeople:

—"The downstate boys come and say, 'Are you Jewish?' When you say yes, they say, 'Oh, you are?' They don't know any better, but they don't mean anything by it."

—"If white girls go out with Negro boys, they get nasty phone calls, especially if the Negro boys are on an athletic team. The coaches don't like it."

—"This town isn't exactly the most liberal town I've ever been in. When Goldwater whistle-stopped here, a few of us had signs at the train which said 'In your heart, you know he's wrong.' Afterward we got called nigger-lovers and whores. Not that the Negroes downtown are exactly friendly either. Every time I walk downtown and pass some Negro kids, I get bumped, shoved, and elbowed."

77

—"I know kids who say, 'I'd love to demonstrate but I don't have the time.'"

—"Oh, the townspeople love us. We give them money."

—"They have huge markups in the stores."

We also talked about education, the University, and its students:

—"A university should be a place of higher learning inside and outside the classroom. This is a sore spot with me because outside the classroom it isn't. Out of the thousands of students here I only know one type of student. That's because so many of us arts students are over here at Van Doren. It's convenient, with the fine arts building right across the street."

—"We had a football player in our geology class; he never did any work but he always got a B."

—"I knew one who used to drive around in an old beat up car . . . till he made the team, then he turned up in a new Cadillac."

—"The prevalent attitude around here is either apathy or rebellion."

—"Ambitious freshmen learn not to care from apathetic juniors."

—"I didn't come for four years. I thought I'd either get married or quit or something. When I was a freshman I lived in PAR (Pennsylvania Avenue Residence Hall) with lots of juniors, and I thought, gee, they're actually going to graduate from college. You're in a fantasy world down here."

—"A lot of kids come down here because they don't want to work at a job."

—"A lot of kids come down here to be with their boyfriends."

—"They're more worried about having money than learning what to do with it when they have it."

The last topic was sex:

—"When I came down here I said I'd never do it in the lobby, but I did."

—"It's humiliating, but there's no place to go. No privacy."

—"You can tell how long a girl has been here by the way she walks through the lounge at closing time. If she's a freshman, she won't look at anybody, just keep her eyes on the floor. The girls who've been here awhile will take a quick peek as they walk through, and then there're the veterans like me. I look at everybody, and when I see something real good, I just stop and watch."

—"It's real bad over here because these are all-girl dorms. One night we were crawling up the walls so bad, we just went out to find a man and look at him, just look at him."

—"No, it's not embarrassing if people watch, once you get used to it. Next week you'll be watching them."

—"In the Ivy League, at Columbia, girls can go into the men's residences. You just have to keep the door open the width of one match pack."

Since it was nearing 10:30 P.M. on a weekday night, the dorm lockup hour, the closers appeared in the lounge to pry apart the kissing stalagmites and sweep them out. Before they swept us out as well, one of the girls complained, "This is a low-prestige school. Why does Wisconsin have more prestige than we do?"

"It doesn't—except in Chicago and the East," another said.

But it does.

Wisconsin is an "eastern" school, which means a long tradition of high standards of scholarship, a history of initiating, not copying other "eastern" schools, a record of independence against unacademic outside pressure, and the tweedy manner. It is tweedy to call professors "Mister." It is untweedy to call them "Professor" or "Doctor," unless of course they are M.D.'s. Illinois is untweedy. Everybody who doesn't have sharp eastern school ambitions gets called "Doctor" or "Professor." Obviously, "eastern" is not a place but a concept. There are eastern schools in the West, like Berkeley or Reed College, Oberlin, Antioch, Chicago, and possibly the University of Michigan.

It's tweedy to believe that questions do not have *a right* answer. A genuine tweedy type insists what's important is to ask

79

the right question. Conversely, the untweedy, vocational, mid-western sorts are careless about their questions but positive there can be only one right answer.

A true tweed will select the most "elegant" among a number of possible answers. The most elegant may not be the most immediately useful; indeed the more elegant and the less useful the better, since such conforms to the eastern and upper-class ideal of the "pure" or "liberal" gentlemanly study.

The thoroughgoing tweed hides his ambition. Embedded in his preferences is a kind of tasteful conspicuous consumption that safeguards him from accusations of vulgarity and yet is more splendid than any number of furs and automobiles. The classic curriculum may be dead, but this is its ghost. Gentlemen—that is, people who may know Greek and need not have to work —go to school for the pure love of knowledge, not to get a job.

Thus, every university has its unspoken tweedy hierarchy of subjects. At the bottom are education, social work, engineering and business, accounting, journalism, and so forth. They are of low status because of their vocational nature and because they lack certain high-prestige intellectual attributes . . . at least in the mind of the university's vanity fair.

They are presumed to be subjects that anybody can master, providing he is willing to be a grind. They have little about them that is arcane and thus are not exclusive. They are subjects to be mastered by anyone ready to apply brain oil.

They lack theory. Their theory is derivative of the "pure" sciences, and not only is this low status, but it makes game-playing impossible. To play intellectual games you must have theory, abstractions to move around and have fun with. Playing games, making work a leisure-time activity, doing something for no material profit—these also are upper class, in conformity with what remains of the classicist ideal.

Sometimes a subject will have upper- and lower-class parts to it. This is increasingly the case with law. The practice of law has lost impressiveness to the academic snob; to him, lawyers are either corporate employees like bookkeepers and public relations men, or semicriminal types, would-be politicians, and insurance chiselers.

Ah, but there is jurisprudence! The jurisprude never argues a case, never takes a dime for a tort—his work is part history, part philosophy—both upper-class subjects. Furthermore, all the unspoken associations the academic snob makes with jurisprudence are as grandiloquent as those he makes with law are shoddy— the Inner Temple, Oliver Wendell Holmes, wigs, black robes, tradition, the Harvard Law School.

A true academic snob is inclined toward Anglophilia. This preference has helped medicine keep up a slipping prestige. The tweed connects medicine with the *Lancet,* and highly favorable Englishmen like William Harvey.

He places in the middle class a swarm of sciences and miscellaneous subjects like sociology, psychology, chemistry, geology, economics, zoology, and anthropology.

Sociology is in the lower middle class because it is is young and the people in it are supposed to be illiterate. Psychology is from a fine old upper-class family, philosophy, but it has lost a lot of its posh. Back in the days when people like David Hume and Aristotle took care of the subject, it was part of the academic aristocracy, but it started to slip when it cut itself off from the philosophers and took up laboratory experimentation, testing, and questionnaires. It lost more status when personnel managers were required to take courses in it, and now the pure tweeds say that psychologists are functional illiterates.

Chemistry, geology, and economics have fine pedigrees, but clever unscrupulous men have been known to make practical use out of them—like inventing nylon stockings, finding oil wells, or averting depressions. Also, chemists, geologists, and economists are supposed to make outside money by consulting.

Anthropology is a subject that lives under the threat of academic degradation. It still enjoys the reputation of being something upper-class Englishmen take up if they are adventurous and creative but cannot write history or poetry. The snobs do not know that the modern anthropologist talks in social scientific tongues and sells his services to advertising agencies doing consumer research on plastic buttons.

In the upper classes we find archaeology (the classic kind that digs up Greek urns, not the sort that spades for dead American Indians), mathematics, philosophy, physics, philology, astronomy, Latin and Greek, genetics, Egyptology, Icelandic, and Italian history.

The inclusion of genetics and Icelandic is not really puzzling. That genetics is a field of study invented by rank amateurs and has enjoyed a fine theoretical development puts it in the upper classes. Icelandic gets into aristocracy because of a snobbish predilection for tasteful obscurantism. It is very tweedy to have a nice appreciation of the Norse sagas.

Certain subjects fluctuate from campus to campus. This is best illustrated by language studies. Ordinarily German and Chinese are plodding middle-class subjects, but if you're not too pushy about your specialty and you concentrate on art and not their usefulness for national defense, you may be able to enroll in the upper classes.

All in all, the aristocracy in the republic of letters is recessive and hidden. You must study the campus for a long time if you are to find the archdukes of learning.

6

Mark Hopkins Revisited

The bureaucracy that runs the University of Illinois seemed to be manned by intelligent, sensible people who were not cynical, whose ambitions were not outrageously destructive, who thought about their work, who were critical of themselves and their institution and were not always hiding what they were doing. They cared about the students, about learning, about the University. Not all of them were like this, to be sure, but enough to be impressive.

Dean Gaylord Hatch in his first-floor office of the student services building on John Street didn't look promising on first sight. A small man with a pipe, in olive-brown tweeds with a vest, he looked like someone who is used to keeping the inquisitive public at bay. Then I noticed that he had some interesting books in his office, like *The Anatomy of British Sea Power,* and Paul Tillich's *The Power To Be,* and that when he talked his voice had a refined fervor to its timbre: "There are all kinds of pressures on the students. Vocational pressures are the strongest, and now they think—it's all in the mind—they need an advanced degree."

"Isn't part of the pressure applied by the institution in its own quest for recognition?" I asked. "When I listen to some people around here, it seems the Board of Overseers at Harvard—without knowing it—are running the place."

"This is a state institution," the Dean replied, "not Harvard. It should serve the needs of the people of the state. Is there a discrepancy between this purpose and the escalation of academic status? I'll let you answer the question, but what really is the function of a university? Whitehead says you don't need a university to impart knowledge, and a university is a hell of a way to do research."

"What is the impact of all this on the students?" I asked.

"The student sees an all-pervading system. We have orientation conferences for the students and we have orientation conferences for deans, when we meet, from a number of universities. I refuse to go because we sit there and lie to each other."

Dean Hatch's secretary called him to say that a student wanted to see him. He told her to send him in, and soon a young man named Larry came in to exchange a few words with him. Just before the young man went out, the Dean asked him, "Larry, have you been writing anything?"

"Not much lately."

"Don't stop."

"No, sir," Larry said, and left.

"He writes poetry," the Dean explained. "To me it's that which typifies the student's own need to do something that has a purpose. One young man went to South America to build huts, and another went to Africa because he wanted to work with a purpose where the structure didn't block him.

"A lot of the activities here are really hollow, and many of the students join in them just to be acknowledged. There's an awful need here to be recognized as having done something, and if you move that same need over a few inches you can see why people are after degrees. I may be cynical, but I think faculty and students each are looking for a validation from the outside. Nobody settles down here and attempts to be educated—more and more they come because they believe they must have that degree.

84

"Now here's a letter from a boy in Paris who used to be here. A history major, wants to be a journalist, but he had low marks. He feels he has to come back and take his degree, and listen to what he writes: 'All this to be a Washington newspaper writer. . . .'

"The real tragedy here is the boy who is pushed in here because there is no room back on the farm; in effect he's been thrown off the farm, so here he is stumbling, trying to find an allied interest in agriculture. So he wants to be a minister, he wants to be in commerce, he wants to do anything to avoid a foreign language.

"I was a dropout. A late vocation, you might call it. I quit high school and went into the insurance business. I didn't go to college until I was thirty; then my wife and two children and I sat down and voted on it. College won; afterward I taught in public school. I tried to be a teacher in high school, but I ran into one of those long, evasive interviews with the high school principal and went into graduate school here. I flunked my Ph.D. prelims the first time. . . . Now compare that with the student who comes here at nineteen and says 'I don't know what I want to do.' He's terrified because he doesn't have 'civil engineer' written across his chest.

"I like to teach. When I get my Ph.D. degree I may go off to a small liberal arts college and just teach. A great teacher, as somebody said, is willing to be forgotten, but here if you ask someone 'Do you teach?' he'll say, 'Yeah, I teach seven hours and I prepare my classes.' He does, too, but he has no time to be Mr. Chips for the student who is looking for values.

"Here the emphasis is always on research; everybody is always studying somebody, yet we can't see the discrepancy between our purpose and our achievement. . . . Mr. Chips again, the fact that man needs to be loved, not studied."

The Dean showed so much human concern I was encouraged to ask him about sex at the University.

"Celibacy is hell. Being eighteen years old is hell. I wouldn't be eighteen years old again for all the tea in China. The question is, are there some standards we can depend upon or do we have institutional ethics? A Christian student can resort to a whole system here that recognizes human nature. In theory, the ideal situation is to say to the students, 'You're here, you're men and women and we expect you to follow general standards.' In fact, though, we have a very difficult situation. This University is no more able than Louis XVI to reform the state.

"Sex isn't the only immoral act on the campus—there's cheating, and there's lots of it. It says on every examination paper that you'll be expelled if you do it, but it's done all the time. I did it. I came into an exam loaded with answers. I had them up my cuffs, in pockets, everywhere. Then I looked up at the professor and I couldn't do it.

"American educators," Dean Hatch said quietly as I got up to go, "while attempting to teach the world, have lost their souls. We have big service projects all over the world, but students without advisers on our home campuses."

Agree with men like Dean Hatch or not, in one sense they are throwbacks to an earlier definition of collegiate education, one that held that its most important purpose was moral. The best-known and best-loved exponent of the college as a place of character formation was probably Mark Hopkins, president of Williams College from 1836 to 1872. For him, grade point averages, credits, and degrees would never interfere with the mission of education: "We are to regard the mind, not as a piece of iron to be laid upon the anvil and hammered into any shape, nor as a block of marble in which we are to find the statue by removing the rubbish, nor as a receptacle into which knowledge may be poured; but as a flame that is to be fed, as an active being that must be strengthened to think and to feel—to dare, to do and to suffer."

"It is the object of the College," Hopkins maintained, "to make men," and many Williams students agreed, so much that his

86

course on "moral and intellectual philosophy" for seniors was the climax of their college days. "The coming year," one of them wrote in 1861, "is fraught with responsibility and yet pleasure. It must tell heavily on our after lives. . . . We are treated like, and feel like, men now and must quit ourselves like men. Soon the greatest mind in New England will take and train us."

So highly regarded was Mark Hopkins that later generations have come to think of him as a complete college in himself, thanks to the most celebrated mot ever uttered about an American college president: "The ideal college is Mark Hopkins on one end of a log and a student on the other."

The words were spoken by James A. Garfield in 1871 at a Williams alumni dinner at Delmonico's restaurant in New York. He was defending Hopkins against an attack by a Williams professor who had said in effect that character building was fine but that learning was a neglected activity at Williams. This comment on instruction at Williams in the early 1860's may also serve as a reasonably fair description of conditions at countless other bookless, professorless, lab-less, underendowed little nineteenth-century colleges:

> The professor of natural history gave a brief course one term and then was called away, so that we had almost no biology. The professor of chemistry gave a few dozen demonstrations and was the only man who taught in this way. He, too, left before the close of the course. There was no English literature save the little taught by the professor of rhetoric, who was far more interested in philosophy and economic questions. There was almost no physics, for the professor of natural philosophy was interested chiefly in astronomy.

The antithesis between putting the first emphasis on the mind or the soul endures, but for the great colleges and universities the decision has been made. If Mark Hopkins returned, they might give him a log, but they'd never give him tenure.

The confusion over the purposes of education today is seen

with special force in the way so many people talk fervently about "the well-rounded man." This is a favorite topic at the University, and they even have a Division of General Studies, which is supposed to put together the liberal education through which a man presumably becomes well rounded.

At Illinois it is the job of DGS to educate those who have not decided on a major or specialized field of studies and to help to provide those who have begun to major with courses outside their specialties. The language of the catalogue in describing DGS is typical of the language the "tradition of liberal education" uses when talking about itself; it is noble but fuzzy, and so ambitious it sounds specious: "Its [DGS] course cut across the liberal arts spectrum and provide for the student an integrated framework in which to see and comprehend the unity and diversity of human knowledge; to understand man himself and in his physical and biological environment; to grasp the nature of his social and historical progress; to appreciate his creative and philosophical achievements." The catalogue then takes a deep breath before summing up: "In other words, the General Studies program helps the student see the world of knowledge whole."

Halbert E. Gulley, head of the Division of General Studies, is a roly-poly man who dresses like a Sioux City insurance salesman. Try as he might—and he tried with all his might—over a long lunch, Gulley couldn't make the rationale nor the content of liberal arts education at the University seem more precise or reasonable than the catalogue. Gulley worked hard at his explanation, like an insurance salesman trying to sell an annuity to a man who wants a term policy, but when he was done, the same sets of self-contradictions, the same questions about course content and electives, and the same nebulous film continued to separate us from coming to grips with the subject. It has been a long angry, unsatisfactory quarrel among educators; it was an old fight even thirty years ago when Robert M. Hutchins wrote: "The college of liberal arts is partly high school, partly university, partly

88

general, partly special. Frequently it looks like a teacher-training institution. Frequently it looks like nothing at all. The degree it offers seems to certify that the student has passed an uneventful period without violating any local, state, or federal law, and that he has a fair, if temporary, recollection of what his teachers have said to him."

The truth is that you cannot prove what a college should teach. No self-evidently valid educational philosophy exists for designing a curriculum, although we can use one academic degree, the B.A., to give a specious unity to an incredible variety of curriculums that are actually the products of developments in knowledge, changes in society, student demands, alumni, parents, big givers, the government, and the European inheritance of polite learning. It was not always so, however; the purpose for founding a college like Harvard was clearer to this nameless pilgrim of 1643 than our purposes are to ourselves: "After God had carried us safe to *New England,* and wee had builded our houses, provided necessaries for our liveli-hood, rear'd convenient places for Gods worship, and setled the Civill Government: One of the next things we longed for, and looked after was to advance *Learning* and perpetuate it to Posterity; dreading to leave an illiterate Ministery to the Churches, when our present Ministers shall lie in the Dust."

The only way to perpetuate learning was to study Latin, Greek, mathematics, and moral philosophy. There was no alternative, no elective, only the classical curriculum which held its prestigious place for the next two hundred years as the credo of educational faith and socially superior attainment. Even when science did fight its way into the schools, as at Yale via the medium of the Sheffield Scientific School, the college would not give science students the classic B.A. Instead, they were awarded a Bachelor of Philosophy degree and were not allowed to sit with the regular classics students in chapel. As late as 1885, the president of Princeton was fighting for the old education in words of obvious social meaning:

89

I am disappointed, I am grieved when I find another course [the elective system] pursued which allows, which encourages, which tempts young men in their caprice to choose easy subjects, and which are not fitted to enlarge or refine the mind, to produce scholars, or to send forth the great body of students as educated gentlemen. . . .

A taste and a style are produced by the study of the Greek and Latin with their literatures, which are expressively called *Classic*. It may be difficult to define, but we all feel the charm of it.

The classic curriculum, in addition to being the learning of the master class, was also the learning of the Christian churches and, for practical purposes, the churches controlled higher education from Plymouth Rock until after the Civil War.

Ecclesiastic control was given legal blessing in the Dartmouth College case of 1819. The Supreme Court's decision protecting corporate charters from legislative control encouraged the establishment of sectarian schools. This case, guaranteeing that once a church had gotten a charter to start a college it would be free of outside regulation, was won for Dartmouth by one of her alumni, Daniel Webster, '01. His peroration to the court has long since become a piece of Americana:

It is, Sir, as I have said, a small College. And yet, *there are those who love it—.*

Sir, I know not how others may feel, but, for myself, when I see my alma mater surrounded, like Caesar in the senate house, by those who are reiterating stab after stab, I would not, for this right hand, have her turn to me and say, *"Et tu quoque mi fili! And thou too, my son!"*

That is why, quite aside from the real values of the classic curriculum, whoever hoped to change it was in some sense attacking or at least upsetting the religious and social order of the country.

A small tribe of savants had pressed for changes as early as the end of the eighteenth century. In 1800, Thomas Jefferson was trying to get his University of Virginia plan going and was hoping to see taught there a list of courses that were subversive to the classical order: "Botany, Chemistry, Zoology, Anatomy, Surgery, Geology, Geography, Politics, Commerce, History, Ethics, Law, Arts, Fine Arts." The idea was treasonable. Moreover, Jefferson had no idea of stopping there. He wanted to change the entire administration of the American college. The proposals for curricular change were often made by men who wanted an elective system and who wanted to weaken or destroy the idea that the college is the custodian of the students' characters and morals.

In the summer of 1823, as the University of Virginia was about to open her doors, Jefferson wrote his young friend and fellow academic troublemaker, George Ticknor of Harvard:

I am not fully informed of the practices at Harvard, but there is one which we shall certainly vary, [although] it has been copied, I believe, by nearly every college and academy in the U. S. That is, the holding students all to one prescribed course of reading, and disallowing exclusive application to those branches only which are to qualify them for the particular vocations to which they are destined. We shall on the contrary allow them uncontrolled choice in the lectures they shall choose to attend. . . . Our institution will proceed on the principle of doing all the good it can without consulting its own pride or ambition. . . .

What was done at the University of Virginia had no visible influence on the rest of the country's colleges, although in a few places like Harvard both science and other modern studies, along with the elective idea, began to win small modifications in the curriculum. But curriculum was shaped by other considerations besides a sterile adherence to classicism. The preparation of the incoming students was one of them: "By the side of the Colledge," wrote the same anonymous 1643 New England pilgrim, "a faire *Grammar* Schoole, for the training up of young Schollars, and fitting them for *Academicall Learning,* that still as they are judged ripe, they may be received into the Colledge of this Schoole [Harvard]."

What it was hoped young scholars would know for admittance to college was defined in a 1754 newspaper advertisement prepared by the president of the then newly founded King's College [Columbia]: ". . . to read well, and write a good legible hand; and . . . be well versed in the five first rules in arithmetic; *i.e.,* as far as division and reduction; and as to Latin and Greek, that they have a good knowledge in the grammars, and be able to make grammatical Latin . . . give a good account of two or three of the first select Orations of Tully, and of the first books of Virgil's Aeneid, and some of the first chapters of the Gospel of St. John, in Greek."

Some schools held to these standards, but with the passage of time and the founding of more and more colleges it appears that, for many, admission requirements were quite nominal. One of the reasons for this was the shortage of students, whether qualified or not. Even the King's College ad of 1745 had appended on it the following indicative statement: "N.B. The charge of the tuition is established by the trustees to be only 25s for each quarter." It was a buyer's market. Not until 1860 did even Harvard graduate its first class of a hundred students, and Harvard, with less trouble getting students, was able to give them a richer curriculum than most colleges. In 1821 Jefferson was writing of the University of Virginia, "We shall be reduced to 6 professors. While Harvard will still prime it over us with her 20 professors."

This was no time to introduce changes in the curriculum, although on both sides of the Atlantic men were developing new sciences and new fields of study. American colleges could hardly absorb the old curriculum. As against the few colleges of merit, there were dozens of shabby institutions lacking trained teachers, students, books, or endowments. Philip Lindsley, president of the University of Nashville, made a central criticism: "A principal cause of excessive multiplication and dwarfish dimensions of

Western colleges is . . . the diversity of religious denominations among us. Almost every sect will have its college. . . . Of the score of colleges in Ohio, Kentucky and Tennessee, all are sectarian except two or three; and of course few of them are what they might and should be; and the greater part of them are mere impositions on the public. This is a grievous and growing evil."

Backwoods piety and sectarian zeal does not encourage experimentation in curriculums and administrative methods. Most college presidents weren't interested. Even Mark Hopkins, who was enough of an innovator to have introduced the use of the blackboard and other new pedagogical methods in his classroom, was quoted as saying to one of his professors: "You read books. I don't read any books; in fact I never did read any books."

Bad as the colleges were, according to Lindsley, students and teachers were not much better:

A leading defect in the American system of education, is the want of good preparatory schools. This evil is felt and acknowledged, in a greater or less degree, in every part of our country. Colleges complain, and with abundant reason, that very few of their pupils come to them well taught even in the few elementary branches which their statutes require, as qualifications for admission. I should be within bounds, were I to affirm that, during my [connection] with one of our most respectable colleges, not one youth in ten entered it thoroughly prepared. . . .

At present, the great mass of our teachers are mere adventurers—either young men, who are looking forward to some less laborious and more respectable vocation, and who, of course, have no ambition to excel in the business of teaching, and no motive to exertion but immediate and temporary relief from pecuniary embarrassment—or men, who despair of doing better, or who have failed in other pursuits—or who are wandering from place to place, teaching a year here and a year there, and gathering up what they can from the ignorance and credulity of their employers.

93

Under the circumstances, it is easy to see why students were staying away from college with the same fervor that they are now rushing into them. The college population in New England actually dropped in the 1850's, and it seems likely that it did the same elsewhere. Things got so bad that "Over seven hundred colleges died in the United States before 1860. How could there have been so many? Between 1850 and 1866, for instance, fifty-five Catholic colleges were started, of which twenty-five were abandoned by 1866. And in the live colleges, matters were not much better. In 1846 in New York City with a population of half a million, the two colleges enrolled a total of 247."

Students were staying away not only because what the colleges did teach, they taught poorly, but also because the education seemed so irrelevant to their own needs and the times. It was more than that the colleges did not teach anything of practical use to farmer or laborer; they did not even teach history or the sciences and could hardly be said to have taught English. Here is an Oberlin boy's description of his English class: "We had six pages of advance, six pages of immediate review, and six pages of back review every Friday afternoon throughout the Junior year. We never read one of Shakespeare's plays or a line of Tennyson." We are not surprised to learn that, in this atmosphere, the coeducational reading of Shakespeare was banned by the Oberlin faculty.

There were exceptions, of course—not many, but notable. At Harvard, Yale, and a few other colleges, the tide of knowledge was slowly coming in. Some new all-technical schools were a challenging development. Traditionalism, plain bullheadedness, religion's suspicion of suspect "atheist science," lack of money, and lack of faculty all helped to account for the absence of change in the schools, but still another fundamental problem blocked curricular reform. How should it be done?

The departmental system of today's American college did not exist. There were very few specialists. In fact, academic subjects as we know them now were in their infancy. Subjects were often listed by the name of the textbook—so-and-so's chemistry, so-and-so's rhetoric, so-and-so else's geology. The subject was the text-book, not a body of knowledge; specialized libraries did not exist. Nevertheless, many American educators did think about the problem. In 1842 the president of Brown University, Francis Wayland, laid down what he thought were the choices in curriculum development that American higher education had to make. His understanding seems considerably more lucid than the University of Illinois catalogue of more than a century later:

... there are three modes in which our present system might be modified.

First, the number of studies pursued during the College course might be limited in such manner that whatever is taught may be taught thoroughly. . . . The difference aimed at would be this: that instead of learning *many* things *imperfectly,* we should learn a *smaller* number of things *well.* . . . By learning one science well, we learn *how to study* and how to master a subject. Having made this attainment in one study, we readily apply it to all other studies. . . . The course of study at West Point Academy is very limited, but the sciences pursued are carried much farther than in other institutions in our country; and it is owing to this that the reputation of the institution is so deservedly high. . . .

But secondly; suppose a course so limited does not find favor, and it be contended that as the branches of knowledge are multiplied, a greater number must be included in the course of liberal education. If this be thought preferable, let us do this. But let us not attempt impossibilities, nor let us be contented with superficial education. Let us extend the term. . . .

The third plan would be to make a College more nearly to resemble a real University; that is, to make it a place of education in all the most important branches of human learning. This might properly include instruction in all professional, as well as ante-professional science.

A modern critic could say that it was the fate of American higher education to do just what Wayland warned it not to do —attempt impossibilities. For example, Andrew White, the first president of Cornell, probably had little choice. He had to do what the people putting up the money for the new school wanted, and the money was coming from two sources, New York's share of the Land Grant Act donation, and Ezra Cornell.

The law stipulated agricultural and mechanical education, not protracted university studies, although it did not exclude them, and that's what Ezra Cornell wanted, too. Cornell had made his money by being practical, by his association with Samuel Morse and the telegraph business; he wanted the institution that bore his name to teach practicality that would pay off for others. These pressures shaped the scope and depth of Cornell's curriculum, and since the new school at Ithaca subsequently influenced other colleges, the Cornell arrangement is worth looking at.

It is easily recognizable as the quasi-elective system we have today. Providing you could meet the varying entrance requirements, you might enroll in either the old classic curriculum or one of the newer sort, but once in a curriculum, certain courses were compulsory. The system, with modifications, is still widely in use and, depending on your point of view, has all the advantages or all the disadvantages of the old and the new.

The new Cornell couldn't have properly been called a university with the meaning the word would have a few years later at Johns Hopkins; and, inasmuch as college was kept at four years, there was not enough time to insist that students go away with the full training of the later specialists. Nevertheless, the Cornell endeavor was a smashing success, and the College soon found itself in the almost unique position of being able to reject students. Cornell proved that something more might be done with young men than incarcerate them, but the old system endured. For Cornell was a parvenu school. Ezra Cornell's money was new money, and the school's president had a reputation as antireligious. Students the school might have, but the sectarian rulers of earlier-established colleges preferred to say they had been gotten by lowering admission standards and by teaching fluff—they chose to ignore the Ithaca experiment. Cornell could not slay classicism. That job fell to Harvard and its new president, Charles William Eliot, whose address at his installation in 1869 cut through the controversy between the "old" and the "new" education: "The endless controversies whether language, philosophy, mathematics, or science supplies the best mental training, whether general education should be chiefly literary or chiefly scientific, have no practical lesson for us to-day. This University recognizes no real antagonism between literature and science, and consents to no such narrow alternatives as mathematics or classics, science or metaphysics. We would have them all, and at their best."

With these three sentences, Eliot began the work of dismantling the classical system and installing electives. Not without opposition. The presidents of eight New England colleges went so far as to ask Harvard's Board of Overseers not to drop Greek as a requirement for the B.A., but Eliot continued until nothing was required but English, and not much of that. Along with the compulsory curriculum, he also rejected most of the rules governing student behavior, including mandatory class attendance. "The *in loco parentis* theory is an ancient fiction which ought no longer to deceive anybody," Eliot said, and the Harvard student was on his own. Even compulsory chapel disappeared.

The elective system was ridiculed, and there were warnings of impending barbarism and moral admonitions, but the victory went to Eliot and Harvard. By the end of World War I, however, people were beginning to have misgivings. It might be all right to let young men who had previously been highly honed by rich prep schools like St. Paul's and Groton come into a college and specialize, but for the lower classes the training was producing just the kind of narrow men against whom McCosh had warned forty years previously. Hence the survey course was born, which men like Hutchins were to attack as vapid; hence

97

also the elusive language in the University of Illinois catalogue.

When Eliot overthrew the classic curriculum, he said it would never again be possible for men to agree on a mandatory course of studies for all. Technical schools may add English courses for culture, universities may add, subtract, and fiddle with new kinds of survey courses, but general agreement is impossible. In education, the course that may be broadening to one man, may be superficial to the next; the course that may be deep to one man, may be narrow specialization to the next. The liberal arts curriculum will always be easier to attack than to defend; nor will it ever be satisfactorily defined or abandoned.

My next stop was at a small house, once a private residence, that was now serving as the offices for a program that was supposed to give advice to the most talented undergraduates. The offices here were like small asymmetrical boxes; I was quickly directed to the furthest box where a big woman in a gray suit sang out to me in a deep voice, "Keep coming. You're almost here."

She was Dora Damrin, the acting director of the Edmund J. James Program for Superior Undergraduate Students (named for a former university president [1904-20]) that is designed to give the most gifted undergraduates special opportunities. This year's top 473 freshmen were in the top four percent of their high school graduating class.

To remain a James scholar, you must keep your grade point average above 4.00, or a B, which is not easy for most students. One of the major advantages is getting an inside track into graduate and professional schools and onto fatter fellowships. Other rewards are unspectacular and must be weighed against the envy of fellow students. A James scholar is assigned a "faculty honors advisor," may enroll in special honors courses (at lower levels this means the advantage of having teachers picked for their teaching ability), has the privilege of preregistration, can get into the library stacks and use the lounges and study rooms that are above Dora Damrin's office.

Shortly before my visit, Miss Damrin had made a speech that was received with some consternation in many of the offices around the University. What she said was that about half the James scholars were flunking out of the program, and about a tenth of them were flunking out of school. Even the high school valedictorians and salutatorians were turning sour; last year almost 40 percent of them flunked out of the program. She also said that this flunk-out rate held true for Illinois State scholarship winners, National Merit finalists, and National Merit Scholars.

One of the reports published by the University speaks, to use its own grisly language, of the "attrition and survival pattern" of entering freshmen. This report finds that one-third of the 1962 freshman class had dropped out before completing three semesters of undergraduate work at the University. Nor was this freshman class made up of incompetents whom the University had to accept to satisfy the state law. Eighty-five percent of these freshmen were in the top half of their high school graduating class and 56 per cent of them were in the top quarter. The next year, after only one semester and with freshmen who had stood even higher in their high schools, the University had lost about 1,000 of its approximately 5,000 entrants.

The whole subject of dropouts is clouded with uncertainty, but the Illinois dropout rate seems to be about the national average. The best opinion is: ". . . American colleges lose, on the average, approximately half their students in the four years after matriculation. Some 40 percent of college students graduate on schedule and, in addition, approximately 20 percent graduate at some college, some day. These have been the facts for several decades in American higher education."

More revealing of the complexity of the problem are the really incredible variations in dropout rates from college to college, ranging from 12 to 82 percent. The reasons students leave are numerous, but apparently only about a third of the dropouts are due to poor grades; the majority of students leave for nonacademic reasons: "'Academic failure' may serve as a device for taking leave of the school [John Johnson told me about one case of academic suicide] when the underlying problems are not solved on their own terms . . . attrition problems . . . involve the students' failure to meet the psychological, sociological, or economic demands rather than the strictly academic demands of the college environment." One is forced to ask why eminently capable and highly qualified students are not achieving grades commensurate with their developed abilities.

One reason offered is that students from small high schools haven't been prepared for the academic big time, but Miss Damrin insisted that the figures offered no support for this. It has been suggested that students who went to high schools that have double-carburetor honors programs for fast takeoffs into college have an advantage over students who had less-demanding high school courses. Miss Damrin discovered that the dropout rates for both kinds of students is the same. There is also the argument that the special, very difficult honors courses which the James Scholars take at the University are what does them in; in other words, if these outstandingly gifted students were in regular classes they would continue to shine as they did in high school. The facts, however, show that all James Scholars, those that stay in the program and those that flunk out, do better in the more difficult honors courses than ordinary students do in ordinary courses.

Dr. Damrin's answer was not a happy one for either high school teachers or university faculty members. It emphasized the difference in the kind of people that the victorious and the defeated James Scholars turn out to be. This is her description of the winner, the James Scholar who stays in the program to emerge, with sheepskin flying, to an academic career rich in fellowships: "He is a veritable paragon of academic virtue. He is conscientious, interested, docile, well adjusted, well mannered. He studies hard—*regardless* of the assignment and *regardless* of his interest in it. His papers are neat and handed in on time. He thoroughly enjoys his high school work. He participates heavily in the extracurricular program of the school. In short, he is a joy to his high school teachers and later will become a joy to his college professors. He has accepted and internalized *our* values and *our* standards—he performs as *we* wish him to perform—and from us he receives our accolade of merit, the golden A. It is practically impossible for this student to fail."

Hutchins, of course, was saying much the same thing thirty years ago:

> . . . the intellectual progress of the young is determined by the time they have been in attendance, the number of hours they have sat in classes, the proportion of what they have been told that they can repeat on examinations given by the teachers who told it to them. Such criteria as these determine progress from one educational unit to another, and are the basis for entrance to and graduation from professional schools. Since it is clear that these criteria are really measures of faithfulness, docility, and memory, we cannot suppose that they are regarded as true indications of intellectual power. They are adopted because some arbitrary automatic methods are required to permit dealing with large masses of students, and these methods are the easiest.

Dr. Damrin called the successful ones "good little boys"; she later used the word *insipids*. She was not a woman to attack the program; quite the contrary, she considered it successful by any reasonable set of expectations. But of this big woman of deep voice and cosmopolitan manner, with flecks of gray in her black shingled hair, you could tell that her heart, her hopes and anguish were for the failures: "They are not such paragons. In high school they subject themselves to the rules of grade-getting for the sake of getting into the university where—they believe—they will find the freedom to develop along lines which are of interest to them. At the University they will be able to express themselves, they will be able to pursue fascinating subjects taught by masters, they will meet other students as enamored of 'real' learning as they themselves are, in short—they will have arrived, at long last, at a place where they can be themselves.

"It is precisely at this point that their academic downfall begins, because the University—like the high school—rewards only those students who conform to its rules. Disillusionment comes quickly. Having spent four years in high school conforming—consciously or unconsciously—to a set of alien values for the sake of obtaining the grades necessary for college admission, these students literally 'give up' when they discover that the University—in the words of one of our dropouts—'is nothing more than a warmed-over high school.' For some students . . . the shock is so great and the disappointment so bitter that they quit altogether, leaving the campus to take menial jobs in business and industry. The common complaint of these students is that they 'can't find themselves' and our common diagnosis of their trouble is that they are 'maladjusted.'

"You will notice that the University says that 'they'—the students—are maladjusted; it takes no part of the blame itself."

Are all these young people "maladjusted"—or are they registering their protest against an environment which has them, in Paul Goodman's terms, "growing up absurd"?

Miss Damrin divided the University's brilliant flunk-outs into three groups: "The first is the intellectual rebel. This student has the audacity to believe that he knows more than we do about what a good education consists of." She spoke of one intellectual rebel who was getting A's and B's as a sophomore in courses for advanced undergraduates and graduates: "Even so he found the majority of his classes boring, irrelevant, and lacking in the kind of intellectual challenge he was seeking. One day he received a B+ on a midsemester examination for which he had not opened a book. This did it. He cut classes for the remainder of the semester, appeared for none of his final examinations, and deliberately failed himself out of the University. Now he thinks he can stand us again, especially if we will let him do a lot of independent study. In his petition for readmission he wrote, 'Society requires this silly piece of paper called a diploma and I have found that I need it for what I want to do with my life.' Such a statement is not one to endear this young man to the faculty. Unless he recants I doubt that he will be readmitted."

She spoke of another case, that of a young scientist who, by his department's rules, had to take a lab course which in his field of interest he didn't need and which he could master with a few nights' reading and a week in the lab. He refused to take the course, and will not graduate. "He's smarter, and he probably knows more, than the man teaching the course," Miss Damrin said in her emphatic way.

"Can't something be done?"

"Usually no. In this case, yes. One of the men in this boy's department called up a colleague at Berkeley, and they're going to let the boy go on for his Ph.D. without his Bachelor's. Usually there's nothing that can be done if a teacher insists on the rules. The same holds true for graduate students. Some of the things students tell you are awful, and you know they're true. If a student gets a bad teacher or one who doesn't like him—a C in graduate school is fatal—there's no redress; you can't withdraw from the class after a certain date. I know of at least five cases of that sort, and every department protects its own people. No one is going to stick his neck out."

When Dora Damrin spoke she exhaled a hearty vigor, a spirit that insisted that the worst problems could be solved. What she was describing was a system that must cut down many a great man who is forever a rebel against the common and agreed-upon truths, understandings, and ways of doing things.

I thought of Ludwig Wittgenstein, whose biography I had been reading. Here was a man who lived to found two major schools of philosophic thought and to repudiate them both. A man who could whistle Beethoven so well that people remember him for it, a lover of steam engines, a designer of airplane propellers, he arrived at Cambridge University to study under Bertrand Russell in 1911. Russell, uncertain whether he was a madman or a genius, took him in. Neither then nor later did he really study philosophy systematically, and probably never could have passed the Ph.D. prelims at the University of Illinois. What would have happened to him at Illinois? Cambridge suffered him when he turned up again in 1929, after having been a grammar school teacher and an assistant gardener in a monastery. They made him a research assistant, which was, as one of his disciples said, "a somewhat unusual status for a man whom many already regarded as one of the foremost living representatives of his subject." Cambridge got out of that difficulty by giving him a Ph.D., more or less by fiat, and making him a professor. How many American universities would have done that with a man who said it didn't matter to him what he ate as long as it was always the same?

I asked Miss Damrin how the "great ones" fared in this system. "The great ones? The great ones have to get through as best they can—and some do, and some don't, and the ones that do move the rest ahead." Past a certain very crude point, she explained, a university with thousands of students has no way of picking out the very special students who need very special handling. "In mass education we have to rely on tests and grades; there is no other mechanism."

The second sort of student who drops out of the James program is the person Miss Damrin called the "social reformer": "These students, when not in jail for violating the laws or for participation in civil rights demonstrations, give first place to 'the cause' and study only when they have the time and energy. Their transcripts show a weird assortment of A's and E's and of A's and 'Absents'—indicating that on more than one occasion they did not bother to appear for a final examination.

"Unlike the intellectual rebel who insults and angers us, the social reformer tends to be a gentle and reasonable young person over whom we weep because of what we regard as the waste of his or her talents. But these students, convinced of the rightness of their beliefs, pity *us* for our ignorance and lack of social conscience. There is little communication between them and the faculty; there is a great deal between them and the administration; and administration is notoriously unsympathetic toward such students."

I told Miss Damrin of an instance at Montieth College, Wayne State University, where a student was allowed to go down south with full credit, provided that on his return he used his "Freedom Movement" experience as a basis for a first-rate term paper. She was not disturbed by this unorthodox procedure, since she sympathized with the desire to keep a gifted student with these concerns in higher education.

Miss Damrin conveyed her understanding of these social reformers: innocent of what the world's way may be, unable to understand that their morals cannot be the world's, the rooted stability of their faith making their courage as disturbing as that of the saint. "I know a boy," she told me, "who's in the penitentiary, a brilliant boy, a fine boy—he tried to climb up an atomic submarine and then he tore up his draft card. When he gets out he can come back here; we've seen to it that he's still a student in good standing. I was prepared to go to the president of the University on that one."

For Miss Damrin "the most tragic type of academic failure" is a third type of person, who has been turned into a "misfit" by his family and by expectations on the part of people around him that are totally at variance with the sort of person he is: "Like the son of a doctor who doesn't want to *become* a doctor, and the daughter of a family that insists that her education must be 'useful' although she doesn't want to become a public school teacher, or the bright young man of artistic bent who has for years been conditioned to the idea that the only worthwhile career today is the career of the scientist or engineer.

105

"These students find themselves in University curriculums which are meaningless to them. Their lack of genuine interest in a field subtly chosen for them by others leads to mediocre or failing grades, loss of their scholarships, severe harassment from their families, and bitter disappointment in themselves.

"These are the students with whom the University has the least patience. It just doesn't make sense for a boy with a college board math score in the 700's [very, very good] to make C's and D's in calculus and elementary science courses.

"Transferring out of the hated curriculum rarely proves to be a satisfactory solution because the student seldom has any clear idea of what he wants to do. He lacks the strength of the intellectual rebel and possesses none of the dedication of the social reformer. He is trapped in a morass of self-doubt which destroys his chance for academic success in *any* field."

Dora Damrin was too wise to cook up another program for her brilliant failures. "I'm simply advocating a little more leniency. We can give special privileges to football players, fly them to California, give them training tables, but as soon as you give a bright student the freedom he needs, they say you are undemocratic. I say forget our sacred course and curriculum requirements." To the rebels she would give freedom, to the reformers, understanding, to the misfits, sympathy—and to all three groups, an elasticity in requirements and regulations.

After dinner I was taken to the home of a philosophy professor who was entertaining a small group of students. The professor was a small, swarthy man, whose clothes, one felt, were on his body to keep him warm, not to show him off. A wandering intellectual, he had apparently taught or studied everywhere —in London, the Middle East, Hong Kong; his accent was scented with the heavy sounds of central Europe. Electric, haughty in thought, indifferent to almost everything else, he was sometimes grandly careless and then irritably exact. Earlier in the semester he had been fired by the University—not outright—they had simply told him his contract would not be renewed. It had another year to run, so his leaving could be very slow, not an expulsion that causes talk and trouble.

There were coffee and cookies for the students, but discussion was what really was to be served; the professor stood in one corner, sometimes leading, sometimes lecturing the students, who loved him. His manner with the students and the Congregationalist minister who came with them was different than the manner I was sure he had for other adults, and other faculty members in particular—it was as though he had not yet given up hope for the students. The students sat on the floor or on chairs, looking up at him and following the discussion.

A Student: I overheard you telling a student to write about what interests him. Why did you do that? It upsets people.

The Professor: (*with mock graciousness*) Thank you. That is what Socrates was accused of doing.

The Student: But why did you do it?

The Professor: The students get stupefied, so I do it. I do it and not something else because I don't want to change the system. I just want to ignore it. It's bad enough that I'm responsible for my own actions.

The Minister: Am I my brother's keeper?

The Professor: Yes, but only up to a point.

The Minister: That smacks of being a Christian.

The Professor: No, no, no—no. I don't preach sermons.

The Minister: My sermons come from *Playboy* magazine. (A few laughs)

The Professor: (*with false deference*) I take my metaphysical hat off to you. *Playboy* is the common text. You should also take your text from *Mad* magazine, but, tell me, why do you give sermons?

The Minister: That's an unfair question.

The Professor: If it's an unfair question, I withdraw it.

The Minister: It's like asking you how you produce a lecture.

The Professor: But I don't lecture.

THE MINISTER: What should I do—sing?

A STUDENT: He'll lose his job if he doesn't give a sermon.

THE PROFESSOR: That's what happened to me. My colleagues accuse me of indoctrinating, but I'm the only professor who doesn't lecture and give my opinion. My difficulty is this: I don't wish to convey my thoughts, and, on the other hand, I don't wish to conceal them.

A STUDENT: Sometimes you say what you think.

THE PROFESSOR: No, I don't.

A STUDENT: Professor, may I turn down the volume? (The boy thinks he has an assent from the professor who in fact did not pay any attention to the question.)

ANOTHER STUDENT: It's easy to give a pep talk and that's what a sermon is.

THE PROFESSOR: It's easy to fulfill a role; that is what the minister does.

THE MINISTER: The role is of a person in a community, and one of the persons in the community gives a speech.

THE PROFESSOR: That is not the role. The role is, by word imagery or anything else, to open people's hearts for prayer. In the Lutheran-Calvinist tradition the purpose of the sermon is that man is sinful and man has to be warned against sin and informed of virtue. Well? You see, I gave purposely a false example so you would argue against it.

THE MINISTER: The sermon is the celebration of community.

THE PROFESSOR: (*pouncing*) So it is, but it is a community devoid of inner meaning.

THE MINISTER: I wouldn't go that far.

THE PROFESSOR: Let's see. How do we come to have lectures at this University? The ancients dictated to slaves, didn't they? In the Middle Ages, lectures were a way of dictating books. Lectures in the nineteenth century were for getting books out for the purpose of change. Now we could televise them. Einstein said he was fortunate that he had classmates who took good lecture notes. As it was, he said cramming for examinations upset his stomach so much he couldn't do physics for two years. Examinations about lectures are worthless if you forget the answers in a few weeks' time. Examinations are only good if they are like driving examinations—to see how a person performs regularly. If they don't do that they're no good. I have a brother-in-law who is a rabbi. His congregation has copied the Christian tradition of preaching. He has nothing to say—you see, lectures and sermons can be very much alike—so he must look for something to say; he finds little tidbits—he would rather not preach—he calls them "a word for the wise." It is the best he can do, but it is a poor substitute.

A GIRL: For what?

THE PROFESSOR: For silence!

THE MINISTER: I preach to build community.

THE PROFESSOR: Ah-ha! (*pouncing again*) You can't get people to cooperate at cooperation. They must cooperate at working together. What you are doing is like teaching students to argue by having them argue about arguing. People cooperate because of one thing: they can't survive alone. All communities that are good have a purpose—I'm not talking about those little *ad hoc* committees that come along.

"In my class, my aim is to cover the curriculum well; so we have a purpose. What is the purpose of your Christian community? What is the purpose of the staff at the University— again, I'm not talking about these little *ad hoc* committees—it is for the students. The University's purpose is not always clear because the University must include phonies; if it doesn't, that will be worse because we need academic freedom. I've never met a dishonest phony, but they cloud the purpose so that you do not see it so easily. The opposite is the Society for the Prevention of Cruelty to Animals. The purpose is very clear cut; if they see you kick a dog, they kick you out. You can't tell a phony in the Christian Church. Now if a scholar is sophisticated enough to know he's a phony, he is sophisticated enough not to be a phony. The phonies mistake their work for genius and their compulsions for the urgings of genius, and that is why some professors don't know the difference between plagiarizing and research."

THE MINISTER: (*outgunned and outmaneuvered, but game with a new approach*) You're the guy that has a captive audience.

THE PROFESSOR: My classes start off with thirty-five and end up with ten. [Dora Damrin had told me earlier in the day that many teachers mark down for absences to enforce attendance: "If the kids don't show up, it's a slap in the face," she had said. She also said another reason for enforcing attendance is that "people say the students'll yield to the pressure of classes that do and skip yours."] Here I'm a failure. My classes flag. My classes start very vividly and then they flag; it's because the students have used up all their intellectual capital. I warn them they are using up their stock, I warn them to stock up, but the students say they can't read because they have multiple-choice tests for other courses and they don't have the time to read. So they go away, and I don't see them anymore.

A STUDENT: (*almost plaintively*) Then it's not you who is a failure.

THE PROFESSOR: No, I'm a good teacher, but if I'm not to be a failure, either I or the University must change. But I won't, so I must wait in the classroom and hope somebody comes.

A STUDENT: (*mildly chagrined*) You're like a waiter in a restaurant.

THE MINISTER: (*joking but moved*) Do they ever come in and say "What's good today?"

THE PROFESSOR: Good question. No one ever asked it before. I'll tell you, in this restaurant the menu never changes, and the reason I lecture at the beginning of the course is to tell them what's on the menu. Still my courses fizzle out for want of homework. It happened with your church course. [The professor had taught a seminar, which some of the students in the room had attended, at the minister's campus religious foundation.] Once you had tapped the novels you had read in high school, you were exhausted, bankrupt with nothing left to use to go on with the discussion. I had a course of middle-aged women once; I asked them how do you explain the quest for happiness to a woman whose child has just died. They were very excited, but soon they had used up the capital of their experience and in a month the course died.

A STUDENT: But isn't this the better way to conduct a class?

THE PROFESSOR: Yes, it is good for outstanding students, and I have a feeling it is the best for most, but it will not work for vocational training, for some of the physical sciences, for languages, for five-finger exercises.

A STUDENT: When are you going to set up your academy?

THE PROFESSOR: (*half replying in kind to the joke*) I have my academy, but I have no students. (*Then with a trace of irony*) However, the bright students have proficiencies so you can get through without going to a lecture [to "proficiency" a course at the University means to get credit without taking the course by demonstrating you have mastered it by a "proficiency exam."] And so even this huge institution has flexibility.

A STUDENT: Why don't you rebel?

THE PROFESSOR: Because the system works well enough.

ANOTHER STUDENT: Why don't you agitate for a middle ground?

THE PROFESSOR: Why?

THE STUDENT: For the students. . . .

THE PROFESSOR: The students like it this way. Look—a math machine can teach better than a teacher. The hatred for mathematics must be inculcated into a student; a math machine can't do that, only a teacher can. I asked a math teacher here, "Why do you teach proofs, when the machine can teach theorems just as well?" and he said, "Proofs sharpen the mind." I told him so does chess sharpen the mind, and he grunted. When a machine can do a job better, the machine should get the job and we should pay the man to go fishing or talk to the students.

It's true the University may not encourage creativity. It may block it by multiple-choice tests, but when a student shows himself outstandingly creative he is usually helped with a fellowship.

A Student: But what about the average student?

The Professor: Well, I object to the cramming system for the average student too. The cramming system presses the book into the brain. I recommend they put it on the shelf and forget it, and understand the difference between storing and recollection. The University thinks the problem is storing information, but the problem is really recollecting it. They teach you to recall in cases of eventualities. I teach you to recall when there is an eventuality.

A Student: That's why we need reform, because they crush people.

The Professor: Reform is very expensive.

A Student: Why does the University want us to memorize all these facts?

The Professor: That's not the right question. What you are really asking is why is the system maintained? Isn't that what you are really asking? Given old professors, it's hard for them to change. Then old colleagues don't want to offend other old colleagues, and so they hire only compatible professors and so it continues. . . . But how do systems change, and they sometimes do? It may change because of over-all public opinion. That's how it got the way it is. The government had a reason to have people educated. The farmers had to be able to read, and so they said, "We'll throw in a little poetry too." The system is now more inefficient than the system at Springfield [the state capital] which made it, but it is always possible that President Henry will wake up one day and say, "Let's make it a great institution."

As of now, however, it is a competently administered University. The administrators know what they want and that's why they get what they want. They don't argue with the staff's impractical ideas, they circumvent them, and what they want is state esteem, so they tolerate poor departments.

A Student: How is the system ever going to change?

The Professor: Remember Plato's law of revolutions—a split

in the ranks of the leaders—but there is also democratic change. Hence the existence of the student senate is justified even if it is not operative, because it could be operative.

A STUDENT: The student senate spends all its time on the things that matter least.

THE PROFESSOR: Those students are realists. They confine themselves to the specific things that can be done.

ANOTHER STUDENT: And anything else, nonconformity, is punished.

THE PROFESSOR: There must always be penalties for nonconformity, but you musn't grumble. Certainly, I'm not grumbling. Why don't I complain about the penalties they inflict on me? Because I can go to a better university. So students who want an education can go to Harvard. It's cheaper in the long run.

It had gotten late, so I thanked the professor and left. When I got back to my room I saw the little biography of Wittgenstein I had been reading. It told about his years at Cambridge before he resigned his professorship because of his aversion to the academic life, how he would start his course (he only taught one at a time) with more pupils than he ended with, and even then how crowded they were because he held them in his rooms:

Wittgenstein sat in a plain wooden chair in the center of the room. Here he carried on a visible struggle with his thoughts. He often felt that he was confused, and said so. Frequently he said things like "I'm a fool!" "You have a dreadful teacher!" "I'm just too stupid today. . . ."

It is hardly correct to speak of these meetings as "lectures" although this is what Wittgenstein called them. For one thing he was carrying on original research in these meetings. He was thinking about certain problems in a way that he could have done alone. For another thing, the meetings were largely conversation. Wittgenstein commonly directed questions at various people present and reacted to their replies. Often the meetings consisted mainly of dialogue. Sometimes, however, when he

113

was trying to draw a thought out of himself, he would prohibit, with a peremptory motion of the hand, any questions or remarks. There were frequent and prolonged periods of silence, with only an occasional mutter from Wittgenstein, and the stillest attention from the others. During these silences, Wittgenstein was extremely tense and active. His gaze was concentrated, his face was alive, his hands made arresting movements, his expression was stern. . . .

Wittgenstein was a frightening person at these classes. He was very impatient and easily angered. . . . I was always conscious of the mental exertion required to follow him, and two hours of it was more than I was good for.

Cambridge did all it could to keep him; the break was of Wittgenstein's making, but even after he had quit his professorship he would come back, as he finally returned to die there. Would the University of Illinois have done as well by this strange genius who once turned down a Rockefeller Foundation grant on the unheard-of grounds that he thought he was past his prime and couldn't earn the money?

7

A Call to Independence

My next day at Illinois was dominated by one man, Professor Sherman Paul, one of the University's most distinguished faculty members with a genuine reputation in his field: Ralph Waldo Emerson and his fellow Transcendentalists. He was a short man whose speech and hard, composed face reminded me of the actor Fredric March. It was quickly evident that here was no mere expert, no scholar authenticating texts, but someone who was personally involved.

His thirty students in his small classroom scratched their notes with ball-point pens as he talked to them. Despite his delivery, which made me think of a coffee grinder, he managed to give the impression that he was standing by each of them, bending over and shouting in their ears.

"Emerson proclaimed in *The American Scholar* a new vocation," he told them. "Emerson said an American could become something new—he could become a writer." Paul said this in a way that you knew it meant something for him, but later he told me that most of his students would probably be high school teachers.

He warmed to his theme as he began to talk about Brook Farm: "The idea of this period was to join action with contemplation. I am related to my work here so I won't go to New York and hang on a subway strap. When I was a child this was a common idea in pedagogy—for instance, I had a garden where we grew vegetables.

"Work, as Emerson saw it, is a routine that is life-sustaining, but not life-furthering, and when work has no purpose it is life-shattering. This is why men put their houses two hours away from their work. Brook Farm was a protest against that kind of life; it was an attempt to build a life with a leisure which invites the soul. The new shopping center in Urbana corrodes the soul. If we enjoy that kind of shopping center we must be sick."

The ugliness of the shopping center led to other betrayals: "I almost weep when I see children going off to school—to be neat, to arrange the crayons—to be enslaved." He unrolled a picture of how an inhuman society can violate the physiology of the human being. He told them about architect Richard Neutra, who said that the human eye finds comfort in the colors of the countryside, but that it will be a long eon before the same eye can find comfort in the city's neon light; about Thoreau watching British soldiers drilling and imagining them as a centipede.

He had not raised his voice, he had not employed an oratorical device, but the room hummed with the call to the individual to find himself in rebellion and independence. The bell rang, the class was over.

Two of the girl students asked Paul questions about an interpretation in one of the pieces on the reading list. He answered them, briefly but attentively. Then a boy cut in to ask what would be on the test. Waving him away, Paul said, "Don't bother me with that. You'll have to ask the departmental office about clerical questions. I have no concern with exams, and that sort of thing. I don't give them and I'm not interested in them."

The boy could make no sense out of what he had been told. He tried to ask again. It was a clear case of his having never run into a teacher who neither gave nor cared about exams. The features on his face showed that he was disoriented, but Paul was on his way out of the classroom, taking me with him.

It was a clear case of the boy taking the professor for a school-teacher and being unable to realize that Paul wasn't going to play that role; he was a professor, and he would act as he thought a professor should act. But you couldn't blame the boy if he didn't have a clear idea of what a professor is. He had probably never been given any pictures of a professor except the usual stereotypes, which are probably of little help in dealing with the real article:

There is, for example, the professor as the "mad scientist," a popular figure in science fiction and other kindred types of popular drama. Then there is the college professor as a fussy, absentminded but amiable bumbler, who serves a half-comic role in literature, cinema and television. There is occasionally a depiction of the college professor, particularly in his older years, as a compassionate and sagacious counselor, but this seems to be a relatively rare model.

The professors' opinions of themselves sometimes seem hardly more promising. The literature on the subject is brimming with bitter relish over what they feel is their low status and their estrangement from their students. They seem to like to remind themselves that they are *the* people in the society who never leave school and who must endure seeing their enemies, the students, leave to make more money and be more important.

Professors may feel especially alienated and rejected once a month when they look at their paychecks. They are not in a well-paid profession, if you compare what they are paid to the compensation for other professionals whose training cost no more in money or time than it takes to get a Ph.D. But paying college teachers poorly and irregularly is an old story: "No small con-sideration," President Sturtevant of Illinois College wrote in

1846, "would induce me to suffer the anxiety I have endured the past winter about the means of paying my necessary family expenses. I am now compelled to have at least $50 before the first of April. I know not where I am to obtain a dollar. In no one way in my opinion is the college suffering so much as from the feebleness and heart sickness which results from the long deferred hope of pecuniary relief which the faculty are suffering."

At Illinois thirty years later, things hadn't improved much:

> After June 1, 1875, salaries were to be paid out of the amount remaining "after payment of necessary contingent expenses," meaning probably those inevitable running expenses, like fuel, light, repairs, etc., that could not be dodged or postponed. Furthermore, the faculty was notified that henceforth the College would not consider itself legally liable for any deficiency in payment of salaries . . . although the trustees would, they said, carry forward a salary indebtedness from year to year, so long as such an instructor remained on the staff. . . . If a member of the faculty left the institution, he was apparently, under this plan, to forfeit all claim for back salary."

It is not the Carnegies, the Rockefellers, or the Fords who make the biggest gifts to higher education, but the majority of teachers themselves in the form of low salaries. It was true in the past and it is true today. Measured in real, uninflated dollars, college teachers are making less than they were thirty years ago. Of course, like the quality and size of student bodies and colleges themselves, there is a vast variety in professorial pay. Full professors in the small colleges get little more than half of professors' pay in the big universities. The pay varies by field. A few years ago a student of pay scales in leading graduate schools showed that deans of medicine were averaging more than twice what deans of theology were getting. Deans of schools of business were doing almost as well as the doctors. Among the professors, the spread was not so great but it was still too large to be explained away (medicine and business more than 40% more than divinity).

The expansionist policies of colleges that have joined the prestige race divert money that might go to paying their teachers better, but the professors' failure to bind themselves into a strong pressure group has made it easier to keep their wages down. The American Association of University Professors, which nudged its way into existence about the same time the American Medical Association came into full flower, has never developed the latter's combination of fancy professionalism and teamster-union muscle.

Lacking a weapon like the AMA, the college teacher finds his professionalism works to his financial disadvantage, for he cannot frame his demands like the hourly rated worker. In negotiating with the dean or the department head, too much money talk is bad professional form. Since there is an ancient tendency in higher education to keep wages static unless there is a promotion, professors not only find their seniority working against them but also may see younger men of their own rank brought into the department at a higher rate of pay.

As the University's Provost, Lyle Lanier, told me, "The Big Ten schools exchange budget and salary information so we don't get robbed." If a department wants to hire a man from a non-Big Ten school, the provost gets in touch with other universities to ask what he is making, so that Illinois' offer is just that much larger to lure him away. Sometimes the ivory hunting works the other way. "Second-rate schools are always trying to pick off our top men. They can't keep it up across the board, but they want the big men to give them a reputation. Last week one of our men whom we're paying $17,000 got an offer for $29,000. We didn't match that, but we had to come up with something to keep him."

What Lanier means is that some schools work on the star system, bringing one expensive man with a big name into a department in which the rest of the people are underpaid peons. Sometimes a school does this as the first move toward building up the department in question; sometimes it's a means of getting more for the money. Often though, a professor doesn't want to go to a low-status school where there are few big names, so if his present school will sweeten things for him, he'll hang around.

Academic etiquette weakens the devices other people use for getting raises, except in the case of the star performer. If the ordinary professor gets an offer for more money from government or industry, his college will usually let him go rather than match it. Even offers from other schools are customarily only matched once.

A professor's fidelity to his calling or his own status yearning can be used to keep his salary low by giving him what is called in the trade a "dry," that is, moneyless, promotion. His rank is increased but not his pay. Yet one more method of keeping a professor's family eating casseroles is by making the tools of his work a negotiable portion of his salary. Thus time for research, lab space, graduate students to help him, or money to carry on the research, are offered in lieu of pay, and the professors often cannot resist the bait.

Over coffee at the commons cafeteria in the Illini Union's basement, Sherman Paul spoke steadily and honestly, but not of professors and their problems. I asked if his class wasn't overbalanced with women. "Yes, it is. Often they're looking for a surrogate father. Sometimes I keep registration open to balance the class. For some reason this isn't like the East where men study English."

He began to speak of students in general: "This generation makes little of its own. Ours found our own avant garde, but here we have to supply it for them. That's one of the reasons I introduce names like Paul Goodman's into the class. They're looking for a mode of life that would be different, not a content, just a mode, a style; our generation looked for intellectual distinction. They look for everybody else to fulfill *their* end of the bargain for them.

"They don't want to pay life's price. They talk about freedom, but they can't handle it. I know a girl—a student—who has an apartment of her own, but when she gets a cold she goes right back to her parents' home. The man, the boy she's living with, went home to Pittsburgh for Thanksgiving to see his parents because he wanted to be sure they'd continue to support him. Can you imagine just leaving the woman you're living with to go home to your parents? I don't know that they do anything sexually that we didn't do, but they have fewer inhibitions about discussing it. They're very frank, honest.

"They want to keep everything open, not commit themselves, keep all the possibilities in front of them. They all want to write, but few do. They talk about it, and the first thing you know they're in graduate school, keeping all the possibilities open and not taking any risks. They're timid, and they have no notion of a life that's superior. That's why their little revolts are so minor. Look at the Berkeley affair; I can't figure out what they're all talking about. They talk about college not treating them as adults! They're *not* adults.

"The students will put the blame wherever they can. It's always the teachers who are at fault or the parents who are at fault. I'm fighting for time like everybody else around here, but I think the student who says he can't find time—well, he's wrong. I'm in my office. I keep office hours and if they come, I see them, and if they don't, I work. But they come to get their grades adjusted, for therapy, and I'm fighting for time like everybody else; I have to be in my study so many hours a week because I've got to get my work done.

"What they think is that I should be a nice guy and come down here and talk with them, but what they ought to do is talk more with each other. A good teacher must communicate excitement, but being palsy-walsy is always a surrogate relationship. Of course, the student's notion of a teacher is of an entertainer; they want a TV performance. TV's corrupted everything.

"I resent students thinking they're competent to judge me. I know some days I'm punk—the material's there but it doesn't come on fire. But they're so critical."

Generalizations about students are best not taken too seriously, except to understand the person making them. The variety of the American collegiate student body makes sweeping statements precarious. Students from upper-class families, students from middle-class families who come to college not to get ahead but stay even, students from lower-class families who come to rise in the world, do not see or think alike. Southern students and northern students are different; vocational and liberal arts students are different, too.

Of course, there have been attempts to draw some kind of profile of the American college student. The best known and most talked about was by Professor Jacob of the University of Pennsylvania, who depicted three-quarters of the collegiate student body as flaccid, politically irresponsible, pleasant but without convictions, half bum, half boy scout: "They are *gloriously contented* both in regard to their present day-to-day activity and their outlook for the future. . . . The great majority of students appear unabashedly *self-centered*. . . . They intend to look out for themselves first and expect others to do likewise."

There are other studies that seem to support Jacob's conclusions. *What College Students Think,* published in 1960, claimed that "Social movements and social philosophies do not arouse their interests or command their commitment. . . . In the slogan of their own campus culture, they 'play it cool.' " But only a few years after, part of the generation that Goldsen and others had called "politically disinterested, apathetic, and conservative" were making the front page because of their demonstrations on civil rights, freedom of speech, and the war in Viet Nam. The question is: Was the active part of the student body always there or has it just come into being recently?

A reasonable guess is that the campus population has always contained both active and inert people, with the inerts in a position of soggy dominance, partly because college students tend to come from wealthier, nonrevolutionary backgrounds. Today's students are tomorrow's alumni just as their parents were, and if Goldsen and Jacob see most of them as nonentities, they are only repeating an estimate of American collegiate youth that has been made for years.

Students, however, are more than just carbon copies of their parents. The Goldsen study, for example, confirmed the long-held conviction of historians of higher education that "campus subsystems" (notably fraternities) were very important in pushing the students within them toward various sets of opinions. Student subsystems have been around for a long time, but they have not always been the same in what they prompted their members to do. These voluntary associations give every indication of determining the more important student values and actions. The fraternities are obviously undergoing a process of change. If they have not all adopted Swarthmorism, bare feet, and beards, they are admitting Jews and occasionally Negroes, and the spreading intellectual culture has nipped them. Numerically, they are less important than they were, since there is now federal money to build dorms, and students are inventing new organizations for themselves. The activist student has more opportunity to make an impact than he had in the immediate past, although he must still float on the sea of an inert majority.

Since Professor Paul was no romantic simplist, his comments on his students added the perspective of maturity. "What they don't realize is that a lot of life is routine in nature. It's routine that holds things together. Life isn't just spontaneity. Even back in the Rockies writing a novel, you have to tend the fire, but they don't want that and they don't want risks. Keep the possibilities open. I have respect for the ones who went to Mississippi or joined the Peace Corps, who committed themselves, but there are very, very few of them. Very few on this campus."

I brought up the issue of teaching versus research:

"In general, I don't think teachers are rewarded as teachers, but I don't necessarily think they should be. If a man is on a campus of this calibre he has a duty to be on the edge of things, to be doing research. He will be a better teacher for it.

"Too many teachers don't keep up. Not so long ago I got interested in William Carlos Williams—he fits into a certain tradition of American thought—and the library didn't have some of his works, a major poet, because the people who were supposed to stay on the edge of things hadn't. So here I am, a scholar who's supposed to be back in the nineteenth century, telling the library to order the books. A teacher ought to be informed, be in the boil.

"Theoretically, I shouldn't be judged by my research, because my contract is for teaching. But if you publish, the work gets seen and the University gets national notice. You get noticed, too. I have more job offers than I can fight off, but the teacher is always left out. He's promoted by the attrition of the other people in the department who go on to better jobs. You feel sorry for him, but the man who does both, teaches and publishes, is usually a better teacher than the one who only teaches, and it's the man who publishes who does the department's work, like editing, things of that sort. More emphasis has to be put on publishing and research, because we're becoming primarily a graduate school.

"Anyway, when I really feel like teaching I like to sit down alone with one student—maybe I'm just rubbing their fur—and ask him what he's doing. The tutorial system at Harvard is great, but we can't do it here.

"I try to fit seminars in with my research as well as teaching. This is where the sciences have it easier. A teacher there can use graduate students in many ways that we can't, but I'll be damned if on top of it I'll be a chaperon or do a lot of the other things they thrust on you—like the religious foundations calling you up to give lectures. I've told them if they want to keep me here, 'You'll have to take this away and that away.' It's rare enough these days that scholars have a lifework to do, but I do. I'm in my prime and I'm ready to do it. I've never made an industry out of one man the way some people do. I did one book on Emerson and one on Thoreau; now I want to go on. Besides teaching, I'm editing two magazines, and I'm on committees for urban studies, research money, and postdoctoral work."

I asked him to explain what his schedule is like. It's a seven-day week starting at 7:30 in the morning and running through studying, classes, committee meetings, office hours, and a little physical exercise till 10:30 P.M. or so. In the summers he works an eight-hour day in the country, and gets in more exercise: "I've got to keep in trim because you have to be an athlete to get through the academic year."

Will he stay at the University of Illinois? I had heard that at least one other university wants him badly enough to keep a professorial chair vacant for nearly two years. "We are a great institution. I complain about it and criticize it, but a conversation like this one reminds me that we are among the top ten on any list you'd draw up, even if we do look like crap when you come in from the outside. The scenery here may not be as good as it is in Wisconsin or Virginia, but the cocktail parties are interchangeable. . . . Maybe we ought not to play academic musical chairs the way the physicists do. We owe something to these kids here—they have everything to learn.

"I don't know if I'll go or not. We are a great community here at Champaign. There's music and art; it's one of the intellectual centers of the nation. We have to be if these old-time free-lancers like Edmund Wilson and Lewis Mumford cannot operate outside and have to give up and come in with us. Universities today are bringing artists on campus—of course, it would be better if they wouldn't insist on their doing so much.

"We are a great community, a kind of principality. Our biggest trouble here is that we're not vocal. The faculty doesn't discuss issues, and our president is always worried about public opinion. But I'm really sympathetic with him; he has a hard job.

"I don't know. If you lead the exodus it's not so good. You go, and people from other departments hear about it. Some of them are uncertain. But if you stay, they hear about that too, and they come up to you—men whom you don't know well at all—and say they're glad you decided to stay.

"We have something I call the Illinois syndrome. We talk ourselves down. Everybody here does it and I don't know why. We can't be that bad. Man for man, book for book, we're as good as Berkeley.

"Go down the list of publications here, and you'll see that a handful of men are doing all the work. But there are compensations. We pay Harvard salaries, but we don't have the pressures they have to resist. Some of our men are turning down Harvard offers. A Harvard professor is automatically a celebrity, a national figure; everybody is after him to publish. They publish too much, the worst kind of popularization. My God, even Christmas books to pay for their latest divorces!"

Darkness had fallen. Professor Paul had left to return to his purposeful work, but I continued to reflect on what he had said. The world is the same, and the words of Emerson to Harvard are the same for all that he said and I heard:

> Thought and knowledge are natures in which apparatus and pretension avail nothing. Gowns and pecuniary foundations, though of towns of gold, can never countervail the least sentence or syllable of wit. Forget this, and our American colleges will recede in their public importance, whilst they grow richer every year. . . . The book, the college, the school of art, the institution of any kind, stop with some past utterance of genius. This is good, they say—let us hold by this. They pin me down. They look backward and not forward. . . .

8

The Meritocracy
and the Coed Dorm

In Joe Gusfield's business they must call him "insightful." That's
a word sociologists use for their fellows who arise out of the
alluvium of standard deviations and correlation coefficients to
speculate on the meaning of the human activities they measure.
Gusfield was a sociologist who looked and acted like a happy,
sloppy man whose stomach and shirt seemed to be tumbling over
the top of his belt. When I met him he was dressed in a welter
of checks, plaids, corduroys, and stripes—all in colors that are
natural enemies of each other.

"The University is a kind of frightening place for the student,"
he began. It has a reputation of not being ruthless exactly but of
taking in a lot of students and letting out a lot of students.
Several years ago our dropout rate was 50 percent but we graduated as many as entered because of the transfers from other
schools. Students are like the cat; they come back. If they don't
get a degree where they started, they often get one somewhere
else.

"Still, it's frightening. Once in a while you'll even get a good
student looking for somebody to give him a recommendation,
but nobody knows him. He's taken all his courses from graduate
students who have moved on. It's like me. I walk in, give a
lecture like a surgeon performing an operation; when I'm

finished, I put my notes away and walk out. That's that. Then the faculty tends to be critical of a man who doesn't pour it on the students."

Gusfield believed that the post World War II university has changed from the old, Goodbye Mr. Chips, liberal arts place of general education to an institution preoccupied with career training. Gone from the center of the stage is the nonchalant son of the rich being trained for a high place in society that has been reserved for him from birth. In his stead is the climbing, career-obsessed young man who worries about marks and getting into graduate school. "Everywhere," Gusfield said, "teachers have noticed the greater tendency of students to work hard. 'Creeping asceticism is taking over our campuses,'" he quoted a faculty member at Yale as saying.

For the new kind of student in the new kind of university, Gusfield had a new kind of sociological word, "meritocracy": "What this means is that students are oriented toward a career on entry into college. They are quickly seeking some occupational identity and feel immense anxiety with it. It means that the quest toward grade attainments is heightened—so many things are controlled by grades. I recently interviewed an extremely bright college student who . . . spoke of the G.P.A. (grade point average) as 'a system of infant damnation.' What goes down on a transcript [of marks] is of crucial importance to the student and his future.

"The student has a fear of making mistakes—a fear which permeates what he does in terms of his relation to the faculty, that new, terribly distant figure of judgment, hellfire and brimstone.

"Colleges and factories tend today not only to look alike but in many ways to feel alike. Grades are the money of the campus and even the very term *campus* is coming to be used by factories to refer to their own plants. On this campus as on others there exists a very interesting custom which carries the resemblance between factory work and academic work to completion. This is known among students as TGIF—Thank God It's Friday. The relationship between management and labor is like that between faculty and student, with one very important exception —the students have no union."

Thorstein Veblen had seen many of the same problems almost a half-century ago:

> .... because of the difficulty of controlling a large volume of perfunctory labor . . . the instruction offered must be reduced to standard units of time, grade, and volume. Each unit of work required, or rather of credit allowed, in this mechanically drawn scheme of tasks must be the equivalent of all the other units . . . these units of academic bullion are increased in number and decreased in weight and volume . . . not easily credible to any outsider who might naïvely consider the requirements of scholarship to be an imperative factor in academic administration. . . .
>
> Such a system of accountancy acts to break the continuity and consistency of the work of instruction and to divert the interest of the students from the work in hand to the making of a passable record in terms of the academic "miner's inch." . . . Which puts a premium on mediocrity and perfunctory work, and brings academic life to revolve about the office of the Keeper of the Tape and Sealing Wax. . . .
>
> .... Like other workmen, under pressure of competition the members of the academic staff will endeavor to keep up their necessary income by cheapening their product and increasing their marketable output.

Gusfield continued his analysis over lunch: "The public doesn't have any conception of what a university is today. They still think it's a football stadium surrounded by a low-paid faculty— you know, Hollywood rah-rah movies. We still say 'learning for its own sake' but we put the pressure on them for grades. We think of college as a place and a period of time in which the student can try to think out who he is, who he wants to be, and what the world is all about, but increasingly it isn't."

Gusfield emphasized the importance of the fact that college education is ceasing to be the privilege of a few and is instead becoming the expected experience of many. We have almost approached the period in American society when you can say there is a college for everyone and everyone for a college.

The mass of students, according to Gusfield, do not attend college to play with footballs or ideas. They come to work, to make good, to submit themselves to strictures of their chosen disciplines, to get the tools they need for their vocation, and to get out and make a living. They come from poor families, from families that have never had university graduates, and they think of the university as a utilitarian institution. "There are," he insisted, "fewer and fewer sentimental ties to the institution that tend to offset it as a means to an end, its intensive vocationalism. The student begins to lack effective communication with faculty and with other students. This lack of organized influence on faculty from student is one of the important consequences of the development of mass universities."

Along with the new student, Gusfield described the new non-teaching teacher: "If you were to ask me for whom is this University run—the students? the faculty? the administration? I'd say it's run for the faculty. And the faculty is organized on disciplinary lines, by departments, so that the problem of total university organization is very tough since the independence of departments is a tough thing to do much about."

The public may think of the college as the basic unit of organization in the university, but faculty and staff have slight allegiance to it—they look to the department. It is the department through which they advance; it is the department that is the local representative of the international grouping of specialized scholars who judge them and by whom they judge themselves;

it is the department that passes out patronage or secures it in the form of grants, research contracts, and special goodies like money to go to international conferences on the shores of Lake Como.

The nomadic modern academic also has a slipping loyalty to the university he teaches in; he can graze on the grass of one quadrangle as well as the next, and the jury box that he looks to for approbation or its opposite are neither his fellow faculty members nor the students, but the members of his profession, his discipline, his professional association.

The department and the people in it, therefore, have a very limited interest in undergraduates. From the departmental point of view, an undergraduate is chiefly of interest as a potential member of the department—that is, a possible future specialist making a career in the area of studies over which the department has jurisdiction. The department must, after all, keep replenishing itself by drawing new students—either graduate students coming in from other colleges and universities or students who are sucked up into its specialized career life from undergraduate years.

This recruitment is very important to the department because to a significant extent a department's power to attract students is the measure of its prosperity. The big departments with lots of students get lots of money. But how does this affect the quality of undergraduate teaching? It could conceivably improve it by creating pressures on teachers to make their subjects interesting in order to entice people into the department's field and thus into the department, but it seems, if the remarks I heard are correct, to work differently.

The tendency is for teachers to teach as though their students had already made up their mind to specialize. For example, undergraduate chemistry is taught with the assumption implicit that the students will be chemists—that is, will shortly be in the chemistry department. The student who wants a general background in the physical sciences, who is taking the course to learn, as scientists say, "the state of the art," its present problems, and

131

its current theoretical development, may find Chemistry 101 completely unsatisfactory if it is taught with the expectation that he will go on to Chemistry 102.

Only the academic bird of the rarest plumage escapes departmental life for full, free flight. These special ones are called University Professors (as contrasted to professors of history, biology, and so forth). Excused from departmental chores, they are part of the University's Institute for Advanced Studies (a very popular device with universities nowadays, often called "the Think Tank") where they are free to pursue whatever they wish.

Gusfield did not seem to worry about being out of touch with students and student life. "I don't think I've been in the student dorms more than two or three times in the nine years I've been here. I get the DI but I don't read it, and I don't know anybody [faculty] who does. The very large nature of the university has tended to make the feedback of student response quite weak. Students here have found it necessary to develop questionnaires among themselves and then circulate the results in order to let the faculty know how the students feel—assuming the faculty reads the report."

Gusfield spoke of flying to conferences in Chicago, Florida, even Puerto Rico. "Sure, this cuts into teaching time, but it's a different kind of a world, than it used to be for a professor. Sometimes I get the feeling we're on a merry-go-round. Everybody knows we're on it, everybody wants to get off, but nobody can."

There is also a judgment-passing school of sociology. Its practitioners are contaminated in the eyes of their social science brethren. Sharp-eyed, missile-tongued, effulgent men, they can be found in misplaced corners of the University, in offices of obscure purpose, manufacturing acrid spit. They are seers, Jeremiahs, intellectual rebels with Ph.D.'s.

Herb Gamburg obviously belonged to this school. Bearded, he had a youngish face, eyes that squinted up and crackled sparks, nervous hands and fingers that tried to describe the ideas which came forth in a humor that clothed indignation. He leaned over in his chair, speaking quickly and with some strain, as though we were plotting together, or he had only short minutes to tell me exciting, just-discovered secrets that I must memorize and smuggle out.

I had found him in an unpretentious office above the bookstore which is diametrically across the intersection from Lorado Taft's Alma Mater statue. The name on the door up the narrow flight of stairs and past an optometrist's office read: The Office of Community Development. On the walls of the sparsely furnished rooms were maps of small Illinois cities like Peoria, East St. Louis, and Moline.

Appropriately, a copy of C. Wright Mills's *White Collar* was on Gamburg's desk. When he was alive, Mills was a much-disapproved-of sociologist because he passed unscientific judgments, wrote a strong prose that any layman could read, and was an emotional defender of Fidel Castro. I made a brief reference to the fact that Gamburg was in a small, heterodox office, instead of over in the official sociology department; twinkling and lashing out, he answered me and the world in a stream-of-consciousness declaration that never heard any interruptions: "There are foreigners in every department, but there are never enough of us to constitute a force. This University? Never have so many got so much for doing so little. We are over-occupied and underworked. Many of the old people say mediocrity has always been with us but that the best people come through. I say the decent people are a mistake. I have the rebellion syndrome myself, the whole bit. What we're up against is the old idea of automatic progress, that everything will turn out all right. There is no tradition of negativeness, of criticism here. Negativeness is a sin for them. I gave a lecture at the McKinley Foundation, very negative. All the foreigners in the audience understood my negativeness, but the American kids were defensive.

"The young were always cowardly, but their ideal was heroic. Now there are so many steps to power which they see and their ideal here is cowardly. We have no glorious, no heroic models for youth. They talk about youth having to come to the fork in the road and make the right decision, but that's too biblical for modern life. You can't see that in modern life, although if you say you do and teach it, you'll get well paid for it.

"Success is easy—that's the real shocker of modern America— it's easy, but it comes in terms that are degrading. They degrade you with success; they institutionalize you, put you in a crystal, suitably mounted, and admire you. That's what happened with Irving Howe, Paul Goodman, and they'd do it to Mills, except for what he wrote about Castro, and they're saying he did that at the end of his life so he didn't know what he was doing. He did know what he was doing though; he knew you couldn't just say it, you had to do it. You had to be in action.

"You can even be an iconoclast and it doesn't make any difference. I was one of the wildest teachers imaginable. I used to imagine there were holes in the wall and that they were listening in on me. I wish they were. Instead they gave me more money."

As he continued, I realized his words could be broken down into a small collection of aphorisms, definitions, sermonettes on life and learning at the University:

Graduate Students—"A strange form of indentured servitude."

Charity—"The University can have charity and sentiment for people, like ramps for people in wheelchairs, as long as they aren't considered dangerous."

Social Control—"Sex acts as a conservative force here. Life may stink, but I'm going to be laid legitimately . . . 'How dare you bastards fuck and not let me?' The kids never say that, but what they do say is, 'I'm going to obey the rules, get a job, get married, and do it legitimately.'"

Counseling—"Counseling is another and most insidious form of social control. It's demonization, and it's used instead of punishment."

The Educated Man—"They are caught in the web of believing there can be such a thing as a 'finished person.' That's why there is mass use of textbooks here; they believe in finished knowledge too."

Marriage on the Campus—"There are two ways to be an adult here. One is get your Ph.D., the other is to get married. You marry your mirror image; love here accepts all social barriers, so you can go through all the motions of having the lightning strike you when, after all, you and your mate were sorted and selected for each other in the cradle."

The definition of knowing something—"I took a course in it."

The academic virtues—"The theorists have the highest prestige here, then come the researchers, but actually anybody who claims he is devoted to science with a capital S is a careerist."

Meaningful words—"Meaningful words, jargon, are words thrown out by you to establish your own status, or are used at you to find out if you are in the clique of proper thinkers."

The wrongs words—"No one punishes you for saying the wrong words, nobody smacks you over the head, takes your money away."

That evening I went to the Pennsylvania Avenue Residence Hall, known as PAR, to have dinner. PAR is a new, pleasant building with lounges for study, bridge playing, TV watching, horsing around and necking. PAR's 1,000 accommodations are equally divided between the sexes. I wondered if a coed dorm would aggravate or lessen the problems arising from housing students and overseeing their behavior.

College dorm problems go back to Revolutionary War times. Frontier community pride, high transportation costs, and the relative ease with which you could get a college charter combined to put the new schools in rural areas where dorms were a necessity. Besides housing the students, however, they segregated them into a society of their own which often pitted itself in riotous opposition to the college authorities. Today's panty raids are certainly no worse than the past rebellions, strikes, mass suspensions, and bloody conflicts between students and the administration. In 1817, for example, Princeton was the scene of one that verged on open war. The immediate *casus belli* was the length of the assigned reading, but one thing led to another:

Bedlam broke forth. The College resounded with yells, interspersed with the reports of pistols and the crash of glass, doors were broken down, the walls were scrawled with charcoal, the pulpit in the Prayer Hall was partly demolished, the hallways were barricaded with firewood. At intervals the students could be seen jumping out of the windows to march around in the college yard, brandishing their clubs and dirks. Expecting an attack from a posse of citizens, they prepared to defend themselves by hurling firewood from the windows. Vice-President Slack, whom they found stalking up and down on the first floor of Nassau Hall with a club in his hands, they drove before them to one of the doors and pushed him out. President Green, after a piece of ice had been thrown on his head from an upper window, took refuge on his study steps, where he stood shaking his cane at the rioters.

The modern college is pretty much wedded to the dorm idea, whatever its disadvantages. (Schools in big cities where there is no practical need to provide housing have an elaborate set of arguments for pressuring their undergraduates into dorms.) Since dorms push up the cost of education for poorer students—who could get their room and board much cheaper off campus—they are resented, but a worse disadvantage is the endless and angry argument over dorm rules designed to make sex as difficult as possible. The *in loco parentis* idea, now couched in the language of psychology rather than religion, is as alive as ever, but an administration presiding over a school with 25,000 students is as much a parent as the War Department is a loving father for a private in the infantry.

Not all college administrators have been in favor of dorms. Frederick Barnard, a long-time president of Columbia University, summed up the anti-dorm position back in 1855:

. . . . *abandon the cloister system entirely,* and with it the attempt to do, what is now certainly done only in pretense, to watch over the conduct and protect the morals of the student. . . .

. . . where a number of persons are collected together, and by the circumstances of their association are disconnected almost wholly from the surrounding world, there will inevitably come to be recognized among them certain peculiar principles of action . . . which are not elsewhere recognized, but derive their character from that of the community among whom they originate. . . . In the college code, the highest honor is not bestowed upon that which is good and right; nor the sternest disapprobation awarded to that which is bad and wrong. . . .

While thus every argument derived from the fitness of things, and from considerations of health, of morals, and of manners, seems directly to condemn the college cloister system . . . hardly, I think, on the other hand, will a single substantial advantage be found to recommend it. . . . That it is immensely more expensive to the public at large . . . [has been] . . . made evident.

Facts further demonstrate that there is actually less complaint of irregularity and dissipation in those colleges in cities which have no dormitories, than is often heard in those country institutions where compulsory residence in college buildings is a feature of the system.

A minister on campus who went with me to PAR had arranged for us to be met by an attentive undergraduate student who explained, as we waited in line to go downstairs into one of the two cafeteria-dining rooms, that coed dorms were far better on all counts than dorms for one sex only: "There's less rowdies among the men and less slovenliness among the girls." During my visit I saw none of either. The hours and visiting regulations are essentially the same at PAR as at any other dorm. Men are not allowed upstairs in the girls' wings, and at 10:30

137

P.M. collapsible walls are drawn across the common downstairs areas and the doors to the lounges and other shared rooms are locked. "I remember seeing a girl put her fingertips through the louvres in the recreation room doors and touch her boyfriend's fingers after closing hours one night," my guide told me. "It was her way of kissing." His point was that the sexes are as hermetically sealed off here as elsewhere on campus.

The meal at PAR was much better than the one I had at Van Doren. When I asked why, I was told that PAR is superior on every count to most dorms. The group at the table said that because PAR was far from the quadrangle and inconvenient to any particular school or college, people who lived there did so, not out of considerations of geography, but because they liked the place. The PAR people claimed that this has given the establishment a special happy spirit of its own.

After dinner I was taken upstairs in the men's section to a floor where there were seemingly hundreds of little rooms, each big enough to take care of two students, providing they weren't too bulky and didn't have too many books or other possessions. There was an inoffensive, sparsely furnished lounge with well-designed modern chairs and tables. Tucked here and there were little study rooms, small but cheerful places to read or chat. The colors on the walls were bright, and I noticed small touches in the design that suggested the architects had seriously tried to make the place livable. Doors to the bedrooms were positioned so as not to be opposite other doors, thus cutting noisy distractions for people studying or sleeping. I was also surprised at how quiet the place was; I heard none of the din that everybody said was incessant in all the dorms.

A deep-voiced, poised predental student invited me into his room. He and his roommate had contrived, by ingenuity and wedges, to partition their room into two separate and private sleeping areas without infringing on the regulations which prohibit nailing into the walls. How they managed to fit all this in, plus hi-fi equipment, books, mementos, and I don't know what

138

else, was difficult to understand. They also managed on this occasion to find room for about ten boys as well as myself and the minister. Another five or six piled up in the doorway, and we were ready for the bull session.

It was a random kind of conversation, in which sometimes they wanted to shock me with revelations that weren't shocking; at other moments they forgot I was in the room and argued among themselves. What they said made an interesting contrast with what I had been told at the girls' bull session at Van Doren earlier in the week:

—"The traffic's getting so bad I bought myself a motorcycle."

—"What do you mean, You 'bought yourself a motorcycle'? Your father bought you a motorcycle."

—"There's still no place to park it."

—"This place is huge, immense. A lot of people say it's too big because you can't get to know everybody, but even in most small colleges, there're too many people to get to know."

—"Doesn't really matter. Everybody has their own crowd, the people you have something in common with, that are in your curriculum—like the engineers hang out together."

—"Yes, they just turn out engineers here."

—"One year they tried an experiment. They put all the engineering freshmen in one dorm. They drove each other crazy. Ninety percent of them flunked out." [This was probably a fairy-tale.]

—"It's much better to get diversity on the floor of a dorm. Otherwise everybody is all against socialized medicine or all for government aid."

—"I'll tell you, the attitude of the students here is hate everybody and everything."

—"Why shouldn't they? The architecture is a bunch of garbage. It was bad planning to begin with."

—"It was no planning to begin with."

—"If we had some trees on this place it wouldn't look so bad."

—"The greatest statement about this place was made by Frank

Lloyd Wright. He came to give a lecture in the auditorium once; he started off by saying, 'I've been walking around the place and it made me sick.' "

—"The worst thing about this place is the student advisers. They ought to have seniors for student advisers; seniors know their way around the place and can really help. The advisers know as much as the freshmen."

—"In the Liberal Arts and Sciences [the largest college] they just run you in and run you out. They don't care. Once when I wanted to take a special course, I finally found my adviser working at his electron microscope. I said I wanted to register for this course, and you know what he said? He said, 'Oh, take anything you want.' "

—"It's what they make you take that bothers me. I'm in physical engineering. Now, why should I take history?"

—"You can't just live with engineers. You have to live with other people too. That's why you should take history."

—"Yes, you have to be able to communicate with people."

—"I'm in commerce, and there you'll hear a lot of people complain about having to take literature."

—"There're a lot of things I'd like to take that don't have anything to do with getting a degree, but you can't. It isn't practical."

—"Man, you have to have that degree."

—"If you don't go to college these days, it's over, and I mean over."

—"Did you hear about that James Scholar—I don't know exactly who—that wrote he wanted to come back. He admitted he couldn't make it without that paper. And if a James Scholar can't, you can bet the rest of us can't."

—"You need it to get an initial start. The paper is what gets your foot in the door. Once you're inside, you can prove yourself. Then I don't think it means so much."

—"You want to know what happens when you flunk out? Well, if you've worked hard and you flunked out, you're in trouble; if

you partied and you flunked out, you go to Southern" [Southern
Illinois University, regarded by Illinois students as a "country
club"].

—"You have to work to stay here. The pressure's always on."

—"You feel guilty if you don't study. You take your books home
on vacation."

—"I feel guilty when I'm studying in the evening and I take
time off to go downstairs to the snack bar."

—"Friday you'll see a lot of kids smashed out of their skins."

—"You live from exam to exam."

—"I've got an exam tomorrow. I'll get smashed either way tomorrow night."

—"The bad thing is they grade on curve, so that the harder
everybody works, the harder it is just to stay even. With the
curve there's only so many A's in class even if everybody's an
Einstein."

—"This place is impossible. They don't give a damn if you
come or go."

—"One thing they should do is raise the salaries and get rid of
the graduate students as instructors."

—"I had a sociology instructor, a graduate student, and do you
know what he told us? He said he felt his main obligation was to
his colleagues and his main purpose here was to do research.
That's a fine thing for a teacher to come right out and say, in his
own damn classroom."

—"They're being pushed too. You know, 'publish or perish,'
'publish or perish.' "

I managed to move the subject over to coed dorms.

—"The coed dorm is the greatest thing since sliced bread."

—"And this the best. It's well designed, homey; it's a good-
looking place."

—"The bad thing about coed living is if you date a girl regularly and eat with her three times a day, after a few weeks you
get sick of her."

141

—"There are certain rules you ought to obey, though, like never date roommates."

—"Roommates? Never date two girls who live on the same floor."

—"After you break up with a girl, in a coed dorm you've got to get used to seeing her around; so you ought to be callous."

—"There's no privacy, none, absolutely none."

—"You can tell what year people are in by where they do their necking. Freshmen are usually in the closets, but when you're a senior you say, 'Who cares?' and you neck in the lounge."

—"Everybody in the newspapers is writing stories about wild college parties. That's bunk."

—"Yeah, all those college sex stories that girls read make them act that way, because they see them and figure they're falling behind."

—"Hell, it is. It's the word *woman* to a coed that means everything. Tell her she's a woman and she'll do everything for you."

—"You ought to come back in the spring and see what goes on here. See those binoculars behind the [hi-fi] loudspeaker? Well, you come up here in the spring and see what goes on out in that grove there."

—"If you want privacy, you can always neck in the steam tunnel."

—"Boy, that's a new one on me. I have a key to the lab. That's easier."

—"This is a nice dorm, though. Its only drawback is it's so far away. I'm tireder than I was in high school from all that walking."

I asked them a key question: What should you do to succeed at the University of Illinois?

—"To get anywhere here you have to be organized. This floor is organized so we can buy tickets in blocks like the frats."

They explained that the more popular events like dances and concerts were tough to get tickets for because the Greeks bought them up in blocks. The fraternities sent their pledges to wait in line, sometimes overnight, to get first crack at the box office. The dorms had begun to organize in self-defense.

"But what do you need for academic success?" I persisted.

—"You have to learn to study. You've got to learn how to cram in a half hour what it took you four hours to cram in high school."

—"You ought to be congenial with your teachers, but know your opposition, boy. Find out what kind of exams your teachers give."

—"That's true. If a teacher asks tough questions, you'll know what's going on, but if he asks fact questions, you'll just have to be an educated fool to pass."

—"What are you scared about? You're a four-point jock." [Student with a four point grade average.]

—"You can learn a lot and still flunk out of this place."

—"You've got to balance your schedule if you can. If you take one or two real tough courses, look for a Mickey Mouse course. Balance it."

—"You need a little foresight. For instance, I'm taking art appreciation."

—"Art appreciation isn't Mickey Mouse."

—"Sometimes you'll get a teacher in a Mickey Mouse course like marriage or mental hygiene who's out to prove the course isn't Mickey Mouse, and then you can be in for trouble."

(Students at a number of universities solve the problem by compiling and selling booklets that describe—and sometimes judge—teachers, their courses, and how they teach. The hope is that this will help students pick what they want out of the universities' phone book-sized catalogues.)

—"Still, you never can tell."

—"You've got to be careful of those higher-level courses with graduate students in them. They've had a couple of years in the subject, so even though they're in the course they're still way ahead of you. You know the graduate students are going to get B's and A's, and boy what that does to the curve! Then it's almost impossible to get above a C."

143

—"Well, in our 300-level math class they've already gotten rid of the poor students; now they're getting rid of the mediocre ones; next it'll be the good ones, till only the brilliant students are left."

—"I'm taking a 300-level math course and I'm scared stiff."

It was nearly 10:30 P.M., so I thanked the boys and started to leave. One of them topped off the discussion by remarking, "And after you get your diploma, you're a depressed area."

In the corridor lounge outside the boys' room we passed several boys who had set up a green blackboard on an easel. Chalk in hand, they were trying to master Cramer's rule for solving simultaneous equations. Downstairs on the main floor there were the inevitable necking couples, kids studying, others playing Ping-Pong and bridge. The atmosphere was about as homey as a home with 1,000 people living in it is likely to get.

As I was about to go out, someone drew my attention to four feet, male and female, sticking out of a big closet with sliding doors. I peeked in, and found the owners of the feet holding hands. In reply to my question, they said they were there for privacy.

The closet is better than the steam tunnel.

9

This Business of Teaching

The young woman had a red ribbon in her hair. She spoke as though she knew her own mind, knew in advance what she was going to say, had a plan of action, but she was tentative about it, as though perhaps she secretly feared her listeners might get angry with her. As she stood in front of her class, about twenty students in all, she nervously pushed up the sleeves of her gray woolen cardigan and asked a stream of questions that might open up the minds entrusted to her care.

This was rhetoric class, mandatory for all undergraduate student at the University. It was being held in a classroom in the chemistry building, but the teacher's expressive hands and long fingers helped to make the white ductwork and pipes in the ceiling irrelevant. She showed an unmistakable concern for her students and for their learning, but in the modern mode. Her style would have been foreign to most American college teachers of the past, as this account of the way teaching was done at Yale in the 1820's suggests:

. . . . For the first three years of the course the work of instruction was chiefly done by the tutors. These were generally recent graduates [you might think of them as the forerunners of the modern graduate assistant] who had attained high distinction in their several classes and had not yet entered on the professional careers to which most of them were destined. Each class was separated by lot into two or three equal divisions, each under the care of a tutor. . . . Each tutor generally met his division three times daily . . . if the tutor were thoroughly capable it was no misfortune to pursue all the several branches under one instructor; but if he were incompetent or inefficient his pupils suffered correspondingly.

The tutors were, however, generally excellent drillmasters. They could hardly be said to teach at all, their duties being to subject every pupil three times a day to so searching a scrutiny before the whole division as to make it apparent to himself and all his fellows either that he did or did not understand his lessons. . . .

. . . . The professor of the Latin and the Greek languages . . . seldom lectured. . . . In another instance he astonished us while closing a series of readings of Tacitus' *Agricola*, by saying, "Young gentlemen, you have been reading one of the noblest productions of the human mind without knowing." We might justly have retorted to these severe and perhaps deserved rebukes, "Whose fault is it?"

If the Yale professor failed to tell his students what it was they were studying, it may have been because it never occurred to him that imparting such information was part of his job. The role of the college professor and the way he performs it has developed and changed as the college and the society itself have changed.

When Edward Wigglesworth, the first full-time college professor, climbed into the newly made Hollis chair of divinity at Harvard in 1721, he had to swear "his faith in Ames's *Medulla Theologiae*, the Westminster Assembly catechism, the Thirty-nine Articles . . . , the doctrine of the Trinity, the divinity of Jesus, Predestination, 'special efficacious grace,' and 'the divine right of infant baptism.'" Although Wigglesworth led his pupils from Calvinism to Unitarianism, it was a long time before American colleges were ready to be institutions that taught more than orthodox truth by rote memory. As late as 1853, the board of trustees at Columbia, a school long controlled by Episcopalians and Presbyterians, was at war with itself about hiring a Unitarian, Wolcott Gibbs, to teach chemistry.

A minority of professors insisted that their proper work was not that of being drillmasters. These men, like George Ticknor (1791-1871), had fallen admiring captives to the German university system in which they had studied. Coming home to America, they wanted changes in curriculum, in teaching methods, in the definition of what a college teacher was. In 1823 Ticknor, who appears to have been the first man to use the modern lecture system in an American classroom, wrote his friend Thomas Jefferson about what success he was having at Harvard with the new ideas:

When I accepted the place of Professor . . . I determined to devote myself exclusively to the preparation of . . . two courses of Lectures. . . . They are both in the nature of works on literary History, of which I read portions to my classes without regard to any fixed divisions into lectures, and as such, they are the first attempt made in this country.

My purpose has been, in each case, to make a course of Lectures more complete & minute than has been delivered before and to introduce, if possible, a more detailed and thorough mode of teaching whose object shall be to communicate genuine knowledge rather than to exhibit the subject in rhetorical declamation. I have succeeded with the students, who have given me their willing attention in a manner particularly pleasant to me since I have declined, from the first, any attendance on my lectures which is not voluntary; the professors still keep on the beaten track, and will not probably soon be induced to change.

As the nineteenth century wore on, the college professor came to regard himself less and less as society's representative to youth, as a mentor of morals and right thinking; instead he began to see himself as a seeker, a researcher, a member of an international community of scholars that makes judgments on the basis of the best methods and evidences at hand. Inevitably, this new professor found that from time to time his opinions and those of the community were seriously at variance. However, dissent on the campus had previously been unthinkable; a college was the last place that people were willing to see used to expose young people to unpopular ideas. Columbia University President Nicholas Murray Butler was only sticking to the older notion of a professor when he announced at Commencement Day, 1917: "This is the University's last and only warning to any among us, if such there be, who are not with whole heart and mind and strength committed to fight with us to make the world safe for democracy."

Many academicians agreed with him, but Charles Beard, then a professor of history at Columbia, thought academic freedom was important for him as a teacher and a scholar, and resigned with a flourish:

Having observed closely the inner life at Columbia for many years, I have been driven to the conclusion that the University is really under the control of a small and active group of trustees who have no standing in the world of education, who are reactionary and visionless in politics, narrow and medieval in religion. . . .

. . . I regret to part from my colleagues. As I think of their scholarship and their worldwide reputation and compare them with the few obscure and wilful trustees who now dominate the University and terrorize young instructors, I cannot repress my astonishment that America, of all countries, has made the status of the professor lower than that of the manual laborer, who, through his union, has at least some voice in the terms and conditions of his employment.

In our day of teach-ins, when professors are leaders of dissent in numbers and vehemence unmatched by the past, it might seem that Beard's definition of a college professor has swept the field, but this is hardly the case. More are dissenting, but there are also more professors than ever before; as a group they still present a picture of a deeply conservative body of men who are much more likely to defend the society than to take issue with it. Moreover, the freedom granted them by their institutions to say what they like varies with the quality of the school. The better colleges and universities will suffer in silence while their faculty members say almost anything, but elsewhere the picture is spotty. Loyalty oaths, religious restrictions, racial segregation, and who knows how much else operate to limit the college teacher's freedom and enforce the old idea that his job is to instill community beliefs in his students. We like to think these pressures do not operate except in southern or sectarian schools, but even the University of Illinois, which is always ranked as one of the twenty best universities in the country, puts a check on its teachers' freedom to speak.

In 1960, an assistant professor of biology at the University, Leo F. Koch, writing under his name and title, sent a letter to the *Daily Illini* in which he said he thought it was all right if male and female undergraduates slept with each other. The letter's contents were scarcely novel and its style did not serve to further Koch's reputation as a belletrist. In it he wrote about "hypocritical and downright inhumane moral standards engendered by a Christian code of ethics which was already decrepit in the days of Queen Victoria." That was sassy enough, but then he went on to say: "College students, when faced with this outrageously ignorant code of morality, would seem to me to be acting with remarkable decorum and surprising meekness if they do no more than neck at their social functions. . . . Such meek and very frustrating, no doubt, behavior indicates an extreme degree of brainwashing by our religious and civil authorities in the name of virtue, to the point where the students have become psychologically inhibited from satisfying their needs in more obvious and healthy ways."

President David Dodds Henry responded by throwing Koch out, and the *furor academicus* was on. No one can spend any time at the University without hearing all about the case; it spooks the place. When Henry got rid of Koch he talked about "encouragement of immoral behavior," and his lawyer said Koch's letter was sent to "start a controversy and a debate"; the affair has gone on until now it has become a minor academic freedom classic.

A few years later, when a professor of Latin at the University came into public view as a writer for the John Birch Society magazine, the precedent in the Koch case put the University in the position of having to be responsible for what the man was saying. Perhaps because he was now a little gun shy, or perhaps because Americans take their sex more seriously than their politics, Henry did not fire the John Birch professor. His not doing so is not lost on the sharper undergraduates who are happy to point out that by his acts the University's president has appeared to endorse the Society.

Just such a dilemma was foreseen by Harvard's president, Abbot Lawrence Lowell, during the time of Butler's anti-German expurgations. His answer was abandoning the traditional expectations of a college professor, of not holding him to the old rules:

The gravest questions, and the strongest feelings, arise from action by a professor beyond his chosen field and outside of his classroom. Here he speaks only as a citizen. . . . If he publishes an article on the futility and harmfulness of vaccination and signs it as a professor in a certain university, he leads the public to believe that his views are those of an authority on the subject, approved by the institution and taught to its students.

If he is really a professor of Greek, he is misleading the public and misrepresenting his university, which he would not do if he gave his title in full.

In spite, however, of the risk of injury to the institution, the objections to restraint upon what professors may say as citizens seem to me far greater than the harm done by leaving them free . . . to impose upon the teacher in a university restriction to which the members of other professions, lawyers, physicians, engineers, and so forth are not subjected would produce a sense of irritation and humiliation. In accepting a chair under such conditions a man would surrender a part of his liberty. . . .

If a university or college censors what its professors may say, if it restrains them from uttering something that it does not approve, it thereby assumes responsibility for that which it permits them to say . . . it is a responsibility which an institution of learning would be very unwise in assuming. . . . There is no middle ground. Either the university assumes full responsibility for permitting its professors to express certain opinions in public, or it assumes no responsibility whatever, and leaves them to be dealt with like other citizens by the public authorities according to the laws of the land.

It is easier to say that the college teacher is no longer the drillmaster of the past than to say what he is in relation to his students now. He may conduct seminars of five or ten students or he may give lectures to five hundred or a thousand at a crack; he may talk in person or he may appear only on a closed-circuit TV screen; he may not lecture at all but prefer to rely on teaching machines or Socratic discussions in which he functions as the chairman of the meeting. He, his students, their parents, his college's administration, and the public at large have definite but irreconcilably conflicting ideas of what he should be doing, and who he should be. Small classes versus large classes (although there is no general agreement about what constitutes small and large), senior faculty members as teachers versus graduate students, "authoritarian" teaching methods versus "democratic" ones; whatever people believe is the right thing for the teacher to do is self-evidently true, but the results of the research into these questions is completely ambiguous. Even such "obvious truths" as small classes are better than big lectures, or full professors make more effective teachers than graduate students, have not been sustained by research.

If you restrict yourself to asking only what does a teacher do in the classroom, the question is unanswerable. On some campuses he is a recruiting agent for a specialized discipline; elsewhere he is a filter who strains his student body so that only a chosen few can move into the higher studies of the graduate schools. His work is as varied as the purposes of the institutions in which he teaches. Some schools are research factories, some apply the high polish of manners and cultivation to children of the upper classes, some are vocational, some are ideologically religious, some recreational, and the bigger places may combine all these purposes and more. It follows then that the idea of teachers all doing more or less the same thing is giving way to the thought that different teachers do different things depending on their personalities, their subjects, and the kinds of students who come to their schools. The idea of the ideal teacher has been replaced; the teacher is seen as someone who may fit one of several models:

1. *The teacher as shaman:* The public manner does not matter; this type of teacher is not necessarily vain or exhibitionistic; he may in fact appear to be withdrawn, diffident, even humble. Essentially, however, he keeps the audience's attention focused on himself.

There is a narcissism (in this kind of teacher) which makes a hidden plea to the audience; it cries out: "Look how wonderful I am! Admire me! Love me!" There is also a narcissism which is vindictive and vengeful; it says: "I love myself. Who needs you?"

2. *The teacher as priest.* The priestly . . . [teacher] claims

his power not through personal endowment, but through his office: he is the agent of an omnipotent authority. . . . The priestly teacher says: "I am valuable for what I belong to. I represent and personify a collective identity. . . ."

3. *The teacher as mystic healer.* The mystic healer finds the source of illness in the patient's personality. He rids his patient of disease by helping him to correct an inner flaw or to realize a hidden strength. . . . He concentrates neither on himself, nor the subject matter, nor the discipline, but on the student, saying: "I will help you become what you are."

In the huge multiversities, which are coming to rule American higher education, the collegiate teacher of the past seems to have vanished almost entirely. The students have become the audience, and the Dean of Women at Illinois can say, "I coach girls on the techniques of how to remind a professor of who they are." And at Berkeley the students at the sit-ins can sing:

(To the tune of "I Don't Want Your Millions, Mister")

> We don't want mass education,
> From IBM machine so blind,
> But just to be treated as human beings,
> Our cause is freedom of the mind.

(To the chorale section of Beethoven's Ninth)

> Make the students safe for knowledge,
> Keep them loyal, keep them clean.
> This is why we have a college,
> Hail to IBM machine!

But fifty years ago, before computers and before there was a single university which might be considered even middling big by our standards, Veblen made the same complaints:

Business principles take effect in academic affairs most simply, obviously and avowably in the way of a business-like administration of the scholastic routine . . . it is at least a nec-

essary evil in any school that is of so considerable a size as to preclude substantially all close or cordial personal relations. . . .
. . . the ideal of efficiency by force of which a large-scale centralized organization commends itself in these premises is that pattern of shrewd management whereby a large business concern makes money. The underlying business-like presumption accordingly appears to be that learning is a merchantable commodity, to be produced on a piece-rate plan, rated, bought and sold by standard units, measured, counted and reduced to staple equivalence by impersonal mechanical tests.

Muncie, Indiana and Harrisburg, Pennsylvania, both larger than the largest universities, are not considered so big that they threaten people's identities. The problem has more to do with how a university is organized than how big it may be; by the same token the organizational superstructure of American universities far antedates the IBM machines, which have had little effect on how they are put together and run. However, there is plenty of evidence to back up the proposition that the schools are run like big business.

Big business provided the money to make schools independent of church aid so that professors were not hired because they made Christian gentlemen out of bushy boys, but because they could deliver the goods in the research lab—an academic application of good, rational business principles. The foundations, especially the Carnegie Foundation, applied enormous monetary pressure on college and universities to set up something like uniform standards and a scholastic federal reserve system that rendered degrees, credit hours, and such negotiable currency at every institution. When this was done, around the turn of the century, there were good reasons for it. Some medical schools were shockingly bad; high schools preparing students for college had to contend with a tangle of conflicting admission requirements; the quality of the training of faculties in colleges was even more uncertain than it is now.

The principles of organization that had worked so well in perfecting the great corporations were applied, perhaps not quite consciously, to higher education. Although there was some resentment of the conditions the Carnegie people placed on their money, and national regulatory devices like the College Boards were not accepted immediately, in general the new practices simply moved the universities in the direction they were already going.

They had already divided graduate and undergraduate work so that the college student was separated from research, the exciting and respected activity that the universities were coming to consider their most important work. Specialization, not of knowledge but of university functions, was already well underway with the creation of the office of dean of students. The deans of students, and the train of psychiatric and counseling services behind them, absolve the modern university teacher of responsibility for the student save his intellect; they also make it very difficult for the teacher who wants the responsibility to shoulder it. The university is organized so that such a teacher cannot easily be close to his students, and even if he is, he doesn't have the time to cultivate elaborate personal relations with them. In the modern university, human relations are a specialized function.

The reference books insist that for every twelve or thirteen students colleges and universities have a person academically qualified to teach. Hence if there are classes with five hundred students, or teachers so pressed by other duties they do not believe they have enough time to teach well, the cause is probably to be found in how faculty is used. Research, administration, committee work, and professorial moonlighting take up time, but so does the multiplication of courses offered. The explanation given for the last item is the "knowledge explosion," but everything that is known does not have to be taught. Graduate students—that is, specialists adding to their specialties—should reach a level of competence at which they can teach themselves. The combining of the research and teaching function at a lower level would imply serious changes in academic organization but might make more teachers available as well as supplying a more fruitful way of learning. Courses offered to compete with other schools or for prestige or because somebody wants to teach one since he's writing a book on the subject are practices as questionable as they probably are widespread.

The teacher who wishes to have his specialized and isolated role will soon find he is moving against the uses of a social institution with a history of immobile conservatism that bankers could envy. The story of William Downes is a perfect example.

William Downes is an entomologist, a "bug man," who could almost always be found in his English-basement office underneath Harker Hall, the small Victorian building snuggled next to the Illini Union.

His black hair was cut like a farmer's, short on the sides, sprouting up on top like tufts of grass. Many of his students—often humanities majors who abominated science, especially if it had any connection with dissection room, snakes, or bugs—told me how much they liked this bug man: "We measure how fast flies fly. He's crazy, I mean he'll get right down on the floor, lie there and look at the flies. But, man, he's great. I'm learning some science and enjoying it."

When I met Downes, my preconceived notions were ruffled. Most undergraduates are apt to praise vivid personalities as good teachers. But Downes looked and talked as a layman might imagine a bug expert would. His voice was soft, his little office disorganized. As becomes one who took his doctorate at Iowa State University, he had no Eastern theatrical mannerisms. As Downes talked, he shooed flies off his nose, ignoring those that landed on the desk.

"I had come to believe my students weren't learning anything. Six months after the final exam they had forgotten about all they had been taught. This year I took these two classes, one of twenty-four and the other of twenty-five, and started them out with a fly of medical importance. I told them, 'Imagine you are a fly. What would you want?' That way we began to develop hypotheses, including two I had never thought of myself. You know, some flies reproduce in high places. Around here they go to a certain tower. They meet there at a certain time, but how do they know what time to go there? One of our hypotheses is they can tell by the angle of the sun. That gets you into astronomy. Other questions that come up will get you into physics and so on. I had no idea myself how much was possible with these flies until I started working with the students on them. The female of this species has three sperm organs. I had known this for fifteen years but had not been able to form a hypothesis that could explain it. Then one occurred to me, but instead of telling the class, I gave them the problem to see what they would say. A physics major thought for a minute and then came up with the same hypothesis. I asked him if he wanted to test it. He said he would, and it checks so far. The work may be worth publishing."

Downes's contract has not been renewed. His students said it was because he has only published six scholarly articles. Downes was not a combative personality but wanted me to understand the situation: "My department head wanted to keep me. My department fought for me. You can't blame the University. If people don't publish, the good graduate students won't know about our department and won't come here."

Later, I brought up the Downes case with one of the people in President Henry's office. He was quite perturbed. He wanted me to understand the University is very much concerned with these problems, and to prove it, he rushed out of his office to return with a copy of the Faculty Letter, "from the office of the President." "If you read this, I think you'll see we're working on these problems."

It began: "The University must accelerate its efforts to give recognition to good teaching throughout the faculty at all levels. It should further encourage the investigation and utilization of criteria for measuring excellence in teaching and for recognizing the promise of continued growth in teaching, so that these factors may be taken more fully into account in the determination of salary increases and promotions. . . ."

But the next paragraph read: "To meet the need for instruction for greater numbers and higher-caliber students we recommend that . . . the supply of well-qualified teachers be increased by the incorporation into the teaching ranks of capable persons not now fully utilized, such as faculty wives and selected emeriti. . . ."

How, one wonders, can the University put out the call for faculty wives to teach when presumably these ladies seldom publish in learned journals, yet fire Downes because he doesn't publish enough? The suggestion is perfectly logical if you start out by believing that teaching and research are unrelated activities, that the true professor does research, while wives, mothers, superannuated arthritics, and almost anybody else are pressed into service to dispatch the numerical hoard of mass education undergraduates. With such a definition of a collegiate teacher and the organization of a university you throw out Ph.D.'s and hire housewives. It is strange, but it is consistent.

The Job of President

On the way to my appointment with President David Dodds Henry, I remembered that Illinois' most distinguished president, George D. Stoddard, was fired in 1953. Campus wits say this occurred because Stoddard was exposed by the local American Legion Post as a member of a conspiracy to turn the school into another Harvard.

Being a college president is both precarious and arduous. Nathaniel Eaton, Harvard's first president, not only got the sack, but was personally abused by Cotton Mather: "Mr. *Nathaniel Eaton* or, if thou wilt, reader, *Orbilius Eaton,* [was] a blade, who marvellously deceived the expectations of good men concerning him; for he was one fitter to be master of a *Bridewel* than a *Colledge:* and though his *avarice* was notorious enough to get the name of a *Philargyrius* [Money-lover] fixed upon him yet his *cruelty* was more scandalous than this *avarice.* He was a *rare scholar* himself, and he made many more such; their education truly was *in the school of Tyrannus.*" [Italics Mather's]

The nineteenth-century American college president had a man-killer of a job. His biggest burden was money raising. The normal method was to make long swings through the country, giving talks to church groups of the denomination with which his college was affiliated. There were few big donors until after the Civil War, but those who did give large amounts were courted. Carleton, Rutgers, DePauw, and Brown all took their patron's names. In fact, money was so tight at Brown, the college said it would name itself after anybody who would give it $6,000, and when there were no takers, the price was knocked down to $5,000. Nicholas Brown finally took them up on the offer.

Lotteries were another way colleges raised money before the Civil War. They don't seem to have been good money-makers, however. In 1812 the New Jersey legislature let Rutgers have one but it wasn't very profitable, perhaps because there were 5,031 winners out of 15,000 tickets sold. Another device to raise money was the perpetual scholarships. They were sold for as little as $25 and entitled one or even all the members of a buyer's family to go to the college free. When these cut-rate students redeemed their purchase, the colleges found they were losing money on the deal.

The job of administering these schemes fell to the president. But that was a small portion of what he had to do:

> Not every president had his ingenuity taxed as severely as Josiah Meigs, who, when he went down to Athens, Georgia, to open the state university, found it in a town of two houses, without funds or buildings, and who conducted the first classes under an oak tree. But in a greater or lesser degree such problems fell to the lot of all. Bishop Simpson resigned the presidency of Indiana Asbury in 1848, completely worn out. For, as he himself stated, teaching and governing were the least of his labors. There was the unending round of preaching and lecturing, besides the practical questions that constantly arose. Finance, law, real estate, brick, and mortar—the president must know them all.

Without secretaries or other help, most presidents had to represent the college to the public at large, be a go-between the board of trustees and the faculty and student body, and administer discipline, a job that varied from gentle, paternal admonition to riot control. (The outstanding presidents of the era were not harsh disciplinarians, and they also seemed to have less trouble with their students than some of their peers.) He also had to teach: "President Hector Humphrey's course at St. John's in Baltimore included fourteen lectures in political economy, twenty-seven in Latin and Greek literature, the same number in chemistry and geology, thirty-four in natural philosophy (physics), and six in astronomy."

The evolution of the college presidency into a form that David Dodds Henry would recognize as the job he holds began in the 1870's. This was the age of the "captains of erudition," as Thorstein Veblen nicknamed them—the most famous being Eliot of Harvard, Gilman of Johns Hopkins, and Harper of the University of Chicago. Such men built the modern American university. Their boards of trustees, expunged of clergymen in favor of rich alumni and the fiscal agents of multimillion-dollar patrons, freed them to develop and run their universities. Powerful, colorful men, often of wide and inventive understanding, they set the policies and did the hiring; they not only ran their universities, they dominated them, made them the children of their particular spirits.

The captains of erudition, like their patrons, the captains of industry, survived a very short time. By 1930, they had gone or were going; size and specialization were undoing them. The university was becoming too complicated for one man to regulate so closely. The very reforms associated with the post-1870 period undercut the power of the president's office. The captains of erudition were devoted to the standards and professionalism of the German university. They introduced it and the departmental system into American education, but the new specialists, ensconced as department heads by virtue of their expertise, turned on the university president and said, "Don't tell us what to do or who to hire. You don't know enough about our discipline to be a competent judge."

When colleges had only seven or eight professors, a few tutors and a couple of hundred students close at hand, the college president knew what was happening on his campus. Today, the president is separated from both students and teachers except for receptions, conferences, and rare office appointments.

The academic leviathan, the administration, stands between the university and its president. Circumnavigating his administration is bad policy. If a president had the time and began snooping around his campus, he would probably only give his bureaucracy the jitters.

In big universities, the people who can best initiate change or try out interesting projects that concern education are unknown people in the bureaucracy. The president's job is like that of the head of a big corporation. He is the university's public face, its voice before legislative bodies and to the public at large. He is concerned with broad policy matters; indeed, they are often so broad that they only mean what the hundreds of administrative people underneath decide they mean when they execute them.

A university president is like a chief of state, but to keep the operation going there has to be a prime minister. At Illinois the prime minister is Lyle Lanier, the executive vice-president and provost. By virtue of the powers of his office, of his chairmanship of seven of the more important boards, councils, and committees through which the university regulates itself, and also by virtue of the strategic placement of his subordinates and friendly allied, academic chieftains, he has a huge influence. His most decisive power is money, since the budget, hiring of upper rank professors, and allocation of funds for new buildings and research must come through his hands one way or another. But the final responsibility is that of President David Dodds Henry, a wispy, balding man with a small moustache. During our interview he was always poised, graciously polite, and smooth—without inciting any suspicion that he was an operator.

For all that a certain tendency to pucker the mouth and a certain overly fast response to questions along certain emotional lines, gave rise to the thought that if you knew him better you would find petulance in him, a short temper or a certain quality of rapid irritation.

As he talked about the University, he conveyed the impression that he had heard all the questions before, that there were no new questions or answers except those he'd given many, many times before. When I asked him about the problems that mass education had given birth to within the University, his first reply was, "I think there's a chapter in the last little book I wrote on this subject." He reminded me that in 1959 he had served on a presidential committee that had issued a report on the topic, and then used several fragments of what must have been a favorite speech: "This has been the heart of the core of the development of this country into the kind of society and culture it is," and "No country has given more to the individual than. . . ."

He spoke in complex sentences without falling into solecisms, but the language was too bland for me to know how he really saw the University's problems: "While the University has been dedicated to training specialists it has always had a strong underpinning in the liberal arts and sciences, and today all universities are concerned to widen general education. I think the changes in emphasis are in method, but I don't see that the mission of the University has changed. For the past ten years changes in emphasis have motivated our graduate schools toward research. We have gone from five million to some thirty million dollars a year in research in ten years. This University is one of a handful of universities that have research competence, that are real national centers of doctorate production, and we're part of that enterprise.

"Harvard is a model and Berkeley has shown that a public university can be a good model, too. We may aspire to what Harvard and Berkeley represent and in addition do many other things. I see no reason why we can't be like Berkeley and Harvard and still go on and do other things that this University is expected to do."

Whether these are grandly impossible ambitions is arguable, but they do lay the University open to a high standard of judgment, a standard that President Henry obliquely admitted it sometimes had trouble living up to. "We have to fight to keep our strong departments strong and fight to bring our mediocre departments up among the best. The infusion of federal funds into universities has created an imbalance toward the sciences, but by and large the infusion has been good; however, there is general acknowledgement of a need to strengthen the humanities. I see no debate on this, we are simply trying to decide how to help. For instance, redirection of funds that formerly went to the sciences are now going to the humanities. In our institutional concern for the humanities, in terms of salaries we reflect the marketplace—unfortunately."

President Henry explained that the University pays salaries on a par with other big ten schools but conceded it cannot bid with Harvard. When he talked about being like Harvard, however, it seemed clear that he had research alone in mind. He made no large claims for the quality of teaching offered undergraduates, but it did not appear to be a major concern: "It is generally acknowledged that the methods of teaching have never been a subject of wide interest. I suppose each teacher has brought into the classroom the traditions of teaching he was brought up with. It was always assumed that bringing in the teacher was sufficient. The University has now set up a new office of learning resources, but an institution can't come to grips with this except by recruitment and making pedagogical aids available. It will take a long time for the idea of good teaching to reach everybody. I don't look for miracles."

What is a good teacher? "I don't think any teacher can be a good teacher who isn't a fine scholar, not necessarily a productive scholar. The idea that the teacher is downgraded in promotion is a false idea."

Where does the individual student fit into the large university? "The informal aspects of how a student lives are very much part of our concern. Our whole housing program, the fraternity system, and our counseling systems show it. But a student can be a recluse and some are, unfortunately. Remember, a university is a collection of small units, and the fact that the students don't know a large proportion of the student body is an irrelevant statistic. I think there are more opportunities to know people in a university than in the small college. The University encourages taking advantage of the opportunities but it does not impose it, and at the higher levels education is inherently self-education. It's a matter of what the student does with the opportunities provided for him. We give him a high-calibre faculty and a great library, but we have no way of forcing him to take advantage of it.

"It's the current fad among student writers to picture the University as an impersonal, soulless giant, but I wouldn't take it too seriously. Undergraduates have always been this way. I could give you a hundred letters from my file here, touching letters from students and graduates grateful for the experience the University has afforded them."

Is it the policy of the University to look the other way to violations of housing and drinking regulations?

"I would not tolerate any winking at the regulations. You may get a counselor here or there who does. Some universities may, but I think it is bad administration. There has been a great deal of discussion about regulations across the country. There's an organized effort to be antiregulation; there are those who hold that a university should do away with them. Regulations are for the minority, for the few. We know that regulations do not make moral conduct, but it is very important that institutions give it the stamp of approval. Students are talking about this a little more now, but I think those institutions which have abandoned regulations of housing life are regretting it."

And what about the other forms of pressure on the student?

"I don't think there's any difference in the pressure today than there was twenty-five or thirty years ago. The difference is that we have a much higher proportion of good students. It's a self-generating pressure in them, not a whiplash pressure they feel from the outside. We are in the academic training business—that's why we're here—and although we ought not be unconcerned about the individual student who can't take this, I don't think we should judge by these exceptions."

I told President Henry that I had been over at a hall board meeting at Van Doren and that it reminded me of some of the descriptions I'd read of meetings of commune leaders in Red China. The dorm leaders seemed to have the same seriousness, the same concern for the right slogan to rouse the slumbering student masses to work. "Work, work, work—you've put your finger on it," he said. "We've attracted a kind of student of high motivation and we try to encourage it. Administratively, the most dangerous mood is complacency. This thrust here for work is the mark of a vital, effective, and, eventually, a great university. Administrators at the University don't work a mere forty-hour week, I can assure you."

II

Joy to the World

It was a cold, sunny morning, the last Sunday before Christmas. In the living room of a small house across the street from PAR a fire was burning. There was a Christmas tree near it and perhaps thirty collapsible chairs, set up so that the face-washed, holiday-dressed students looked at one another as they sang a Christmas carol. They were accompanied by several students playing recorders. It was the Christmas service at the "chapel-center" of the United Christian Fellowship, a joint ministry of five big denominations, that serves the students in the dorms that are too far from religious foundations for easy and informal access. It seemed more like family prayers than church, with everybody so close together, no pulpit, and the minister standing by the side of the fireplace.

In the foyer outside the living-room doorway were Ed Nestingen, director of the campus YMCA, and a philosophy professor, Harry Tiebout, a tall, thin man with sharp features who had a wide reputation as a good teacher.

The recorders piped their last note, and the two men started into the living room. The minister explained to the students that Nestingen and Tiebout would read and comment on W. H. Auden's Christmas Oratorio *For the Time Being,* and the two men climbed up on high draftsmen stools. Of the two, Tiebout was the dominant one, the better reader, the better dramatist. Nestingen backed him up during the running commentary on the piece, but Tiebout did most of the talking. He began by asking, "How many of you have read it?" No one had. Tiebout was unconcerned; apparently he had expected that few, if any, would be familiar with the poem. He was preeminently the teacher; as willing to teach in the church as in the classroom, or in the streets.

"This is an extremely complex poem," he told them. "It will either shock or disgust you, because it talks about Christmas in an earthy way you have never heard before. Religion in the world has always had one of two purposes: either to make good citizens out of merry pagans, make the trains run on time, and the computers whine; or, the other purpose, which is disorganized and Christian. It is the religion of the submerged id. This religion is the spontaneity and creativity in us, and this Christianity commands that you should love the id as much as you love the superego.

"Auden is saying that the Incarnation is the voice of the id, the tiger in the forest, the scatological principle. It is earthy and vital and always with us, no matter how much we may push it down, and that's why he says of it—and this may shock you:

> Perhaps that mysterious noise at the back of the brain
> We noticed on certain occasions—sitting alone
> In the waiting room of the country junction, looking
> Up at the toilet window—was not indigestion
> But this horror starting already to scratch its way in?

"The It, the horror, is the power of creativity which Auden couples with the earth and earthy things. It is the very opposite of the button-down collar, the five-point hero marrying the homecoming queen, living in a bungalow and having beautiful children who all get athletic scholarships to the University of Illinois."

They began to read, not the whole piece—which is too long—but generous slices, taking turns as the chorus and the various actors. It was impossible to guess what the students might be thinking, but they were absorbed. There was no wiggling or scraping of feet, not even coughs and sniffles, as the words came out with unforeseen, direct, and surprising application to their lives.

Tiebout began a kind of running commentary on Herod's lines: "Herod sees the Incarnation and the fuss over it as the revolt of the kooks which will lead to chaos taking over. Herod says, 'Because the decision must be in conformity with Nature and Necessity,' but does anyone know how to be in conformity with nature and necessity? Does Lyndon Johnson?"

They came to the end, the most famous lines of the poem which begin:

Well, so that is that. Now we must dismantle the tree,
Putting the decorations back into their cardboard boxes. . . .

Some of the students, recognizing themselves and their families, laughed softly, but some did not, like the fair-haired girl in the green dress who nodded her head in a sad and penitential recognition of the words' meaning.

The minister waited about thirty seconds and then said, "One of the things that blocks congregational response is the final hymn; let's not have the final hymn, but some response."

Tiebout disagreed. "How about 'Joy to the World?' That's a good hymn."

"There may be responses," the minister responded, anxious lest the least desire on the part of any student to step out of the crowd not be thwarted.

"Let's do both," suggested Tiebout. "Anybody want to say something? Ask a question. You can't talk looking at each other."

"I feel sort of cheated," a girl said very slowly, thinking out her meaning with great care. "It tears down everything we believe in, but it doesn't say what to do. It picks you up and puts you down in the same place."

"Yes," Tiebout answered, "it does what the therapist or Zen does. I had a student once who said that at the beginning when he was studying Zen the mountain wasn't the mountain, and the river wasn't the river, but as he understood more the mountain was the mountain and the river was the river. Outwardly you are the same, life is the same, but inwardly there is a difference. You could also say that the poem is a revolt in the name of creativity against order, but it can't be taken by itself. You can only approach this revolt through the ordinary forms of life, in a religious way, as a puritan—Zen. The horror of it all is that there must be a crucifixion of all ideals, of all rational plans, but still I don't want you to think you don't have to go back to the dorm and crack a book. That's all still there."

They sang "Joy to the World," and the students went back to the dorms. Everybody left but the minister, Tiebout, and I. I asked the minister if the people who put up the money for the chapel knew that Auden and sedition were being preached from the pulpit.

"Basically," he replied, "the denominational sponsors want the seats filled. They want the students taught not to steal or destroy property, but whatever you want to say about these kids, at least they're willing to sit through something like Auden without raising an arm of rebellion, and that is more than you can say about most congregations. If they're going to reject Christianity, let them reject the real thing, and not whatever it is they get pumped into them back home at church."

Tiebout shook his head regretfully. "I don't know if we should have read them that Auden."

"Why not?"

"That poem is very dangerous when it's taken out of context. God, some of these kids want to study Zen Buddhism, but what if they think it means sitting still in a trance or lying in bed in their dorms? They're looking to be taken up high, transposed from the coffee house to the convent where they can wear a coif or get some kind of badge telling them life is what life is.

"I hope you're not taking all this down; I already have a reputation as the campus nut. I'm supposed to be a radical stimulator of ideas and also the head of the Democratic party. People remember things I said years ago, so I've become neurotically defensive about saying radical things. God knows what those kids are going to do with that poem, or what they think it means."

"It's an atom in the students' total experience. It won't affect them that much," the minister assured him.

As Tiebout waited for a phone call from a local politician, he expanded on the problems of getting an education at Illinois. "If you know where the good guys are, you can get a good education here. You've got to stay out of all the Mickey Mouse activities they have, and find the good men. The problem is to concentrate the liberal arts students so they can begin to produce an environment in which the students and the good professors live together. Curiously enough, the YMCA does that in a way. The YMCA is the center of student intellectual activities. Naturally it is supported by fat cats who want to keep the kids away from sex and labor unions, but the people who run it have other ideas. That's the way it always is.

"But what I want to know is where are the young nuts? The new guys come in filled with passion and enthusiasm and after two or three years they slow down and shut up. I don't see why you have to put all this in the book.

"Students don't show up for anything here—nothing. You have to shock them with an electric stick. This is a technical school, that's what it's famous for, that and its fraternities. You've got to dissipate the atmosphere they throw off, but we have a communications problem that's insuperable. To get a good education here you have to stay out of the Greek system and know how to find companions. That's part of the communication problem."

The minister cut in. "One of the things we are trying to do to overcome that is starting discussion tables in the dorm. We discuss a play or a book and then that becomes the topic of my sermon the next Sunday."

"Another thing you can do," Tiebout said, "is you can prohibit students going home on weekends. They're never around for University functions, and the most important education is outside of the classroom, concerts, discussions, parties. They go home to their suburbs and small towns and get completely re-integrated into their family lives so that all the progress they've made during the week is lost. They become provincial little sons and daughters again. Oh God, where are the young nuts coming up? Isn't there anybody else? I'm getting old. Well, there's a new guy in the Math Department I've been watching. He's got that glazed look in his eye. I have hopes for him."

The Sunday afternoon antiphony was being sung by the Slob Contingent as they drank coffee in the Tavern, the snack shop in the basement of the Union. I sat down at their table next to a girl with a heart-shaped face; the brown eyes had fear in them and the tiny mouth assumed a sour pout when she was not talking. Her name was Melinda: "I want to get out of this place. I feel I have no mind, but my father would kill me if I withdrew. I hate the place but I don't want to leave the people. I love the people."

She told me she was going to a psychiatrist. "I didn't go to some classes. I cut mechanical drawing and some other classes. Why should I go? I asked the mechanical drawing teacher 'Why do I need to take this if I'm going to be a painter?' He said, 'It's required.' That's why I hate this place. You ask a question and they say, 'It's required.' It's the rules but they never say why. And rhetoric is a stupid class. The students don't read the assignments and they don't answer the questions. So I cut."

"But how did you end up at the psychiatrist's?"

"My rhet teacher sent a note over to the dorm saying I hadn't been coming to class. So they started watching me."

"What do you mean, they started watching you?"

"You know. The GA [Graduate Assistant; they have one on every floor of all the dorms] asked a lot of questions. They asked my roommate things like who my friends in the dorm were, and they'd come in and ask my roommate 'Where is she? What's she doing?' They'd bring me downstairs to have nightly 'chats' with the counselors and ask me about my life. They were very kind but they don't have any right to ask me questions like that.

"One day I went to see the doctor. I was tired. I cried. He sent me to see a counselor and they [student counseling] said I'd better see a psychiatrist."

The other Slob Contingenteers present, six or seven of them, warned Melinda to be careful of what she said to the psychiatrist because, they assured her, he would violate professional confidences and "fink to the administration." Why, I asked them, would the administration want to know what Melinda tells her psychiatrist?

They said that the administration wanted information on politically dissident students so they can blackball them out of the Peace Corps or graduate schools, and also as a means of getting a line on drug activities. "Like," says one, "the party the other night that got stopped by the cops because a girl took two stomach pills."

"Hell, they stopped that party because somebody was mainlining in the back room."

"She wasn't."

"Yes, she was. She was shooting into her wrist."

"Jesus Christ, that shows you what you know. You don't mainline into your wrist, you mainline on the inside of your upper forearm."

"It happens that sometimes you can get the vein better in the wrist."

"Anyway, she was taking stomach pills."

Before they can go around the topic a second time, I ask Melinda why she is a member of the Slob Contingent.

"The Slob Contingent is the best thing I've found at this University."

"The only attraction the Slob Contingent's members have for each other," a boy put in, "is that they dislike each other less than they dislike everybody else. Our major occupation is nothing. We don't do anything. We sit and we dislike people."

There was a fine rhetoric appeal in the last sentence. You could see it catch hold of the imaginations around the table. They each wished to say something telling and they did, one after the other, but not rapidly. They spoke in grave series as Indians in the circular council are supposed to speak their pieces:

—"There is nothing but boredom to hope for from a University that does not have *Naked Lunch* in its card catalogue."

—"One of the big jollies is that the people you see before you are the people who have all been rejected by the college of their choice."

—"The scene I would have like to have made was Paris in the 1890's with Zola and all those other guys digging each other and turning out great stuff."

—"I've waited at the castle door. I've had the writing machine write unintelligible words on my back." (This last a reference to Franz Kafka's, *The Castle*.)

—"Ennui shall overcome."

On Sunday night ODK, the University honor society, met in Professor Wallace's living room. The society's president, Elliott Peskind, a nice young man from the School of Commerce, told me it rotated its meetings at different professors' homes in order to benefit from the informal atmosphere and to make discussion freer. Nevertheless, the mood was restrained as thirteen students, two professors, and two deans gradually took their seats. Everyone wore a shirt and tie; three students dared sports coats, and two wore brown shoes instead of black.

You have to be a cracking good student to be elected to ODK;

the students present, therefore, were the University's judgment of its very best. The fact that Dean Robert Rogers, who presides over the most important and largest college at the University, Liberal Arts and Sciences, would give his Sunday evening to this meeting, was an indication of the esteem in which the society is held.

As chairman, Elliott Peskind guided the meeting to agreement on minor business and moved quickly to the major concerns of the evening: "Since this is a discussion group where we are supposed to exchange information and stimulate each other by discussing pertinent articles we might have read, I thought I might mention one that I found very interesting in the *Saturday Review of Literature*. It was on technology's challenge to education. I found it very interesting, stimulating. Has anybody else read anything or has an article they might want to bring to our attention?" There was not so much as a grunt to help out the valiant Peskind, although faculty and deans managed small nodding gestures to indicate approval of "outside reading." Peskind resumed: "In that case I think I should introduce our speaker for this evening. He needs no introduction both as a distinguished scholar of excellence and a creative administrator. Dean Rogers is going to speak to us about foreign studies."

"At Illinois," the Dean began, "one of the oldest programs in foreign studies is our program in Latin-American studies, which to my knowledge goes back to 1948." The Dean talked about that awhile and then moved on to the center for Russian studies and the grant from the Doris Duke Foundation which made it possible. "In 1961, President Henry held a special faculty conference which was to deal with the extent the University should become involved in non-Western studies." The conference's result was that "the program in linguistics became a department and we began to offer programs in the so-called exotic languages." Next, the Dean explained that the Ford Foundation had given the University a grant for a new center for Asian studies, but, he added, they seemed to be having difficulties getting teachers:

"One effort made without much success so far, has been to infuse non-Western material into other courses. It had been hoped, for instance, that Chinese and Japanese drama might be infused into some general literature course for comparative purposes." That hadn't worked out too well, so another conference "for more infusion" had been held, but it now appeared that non-Western studies would be specialized.

The next question Dean Rogers took up was that of University of Illinois students studying abroad. The main burden of his remarks was negative: "Some programs of study overseas are designed to improve the social finesse of students participating in them, but whatever the object, study abroad presents a number of problems that have not yet been solved.

"European universities are usually graduate schools, and the average American undergraduate is not the intellectual equal of the European university student. There is a chasm between the professor and the student; the professor appears and gives his lecture and that's the end of it. We think we have a problem here, but by comparison, our student-professor relationship is one of the utmost intimacy. Foreign universities cannot comprehend our credit system. Some American universities send supervisors to arrange academic credits and to make sure the French professors do their job. French professors only teach the American students for the additional sum of money they earn by doing so. The French professor will come for fifty minutes, give his lecture, and leave; he has no interest in the students and if he is required to give an examination, he'll let somebody else do it and then he'll give everybody an A!"

During the question period, one of the students politely asked if there might not be some good reason for studying abroad. Dean Rogers was basically unyielding:

"I think anyone will get better formal instruction by staying at his home university, but you *can* argue that not all education is in the classroom. Nevertheless, the advantages of studying abroad are only a certain sophistication and some language experience. French students go off to their separate groups and are not about to accept American students generally. You can see the same thing here, how the foreign students generally stay by themselves at the University of Illinois."

Foreigners' clannishness was not the only danger: "It takes a good deal of stamina for the American student abroad. They're not checked up on there and the freedom they get demands a good deal of stamina. It probably ruins more students than it helps, and then, as I said, French universities, and Austrian and German too, say you can't expect as much from American students and pass all of them."

The students looked rather subdued; there were a few false starts and everyone was relieved when the other dean in the room started to talk. This was Dean Weller of the College of Fine and Applied Arts. He had almost no hair but apparently possessed both a sense of humor and a hopeful opinion about associating with foreigners. "Our college was offered a glamorous place on the Riviera," he remarked. "It's like a Hollywood movie set and one of the best restaurants in France is down the road. It probably isn't the best location to study French art and architecture, but we're making the rounds of the foundations—hoping we can get enough money to open it up." He went on to mention that his son had studied a year in Florence, living with an Italian family, with full credit and without any noticeably unfortunate side effects.

Discussion dwindled, talk became more general, and our host brought out chicken sandwiches, cookies, and coffee. While the eating went on, there were genteel efforts by people of different specializations to try to find points in common. The professor of geology told John Johnson that he thought geology and John's field, physics, now had a common boundary. John agreed, and they talked for a while about "space lattices" and about crystals. A few minutes later everyone had said thank you and good-bye.

On our way back to the campus, Elliott Peskind was apologetic about the evening, saying that their meetings are usually livelier

177

and the people more forthright, but he and the other boy in the car were depressed about what Rogers had said. We went to the commons for coffee where Peskind, who was active in his own fraternity, ZBT, suggested that fraternities were becoming more academically minded and that if they did not they would be out of business. He said that if you are a Greek you can go further on the campus with less ability, because you have a claque behind you that knows your name and will push you. He also spoke disparagingly of such Greek-dominated celebrations as "King-Dad," "when a guy who is elected top dad gets a coronation like the one they gave Edward VII."

What was more depressing, however, was that a senior like Peskind, the president of the honor society, could look back at his college career and say, as he did, "I feel that for three years here my ability has been wasted."

12

Big Institutions
Can Scare Anybody

"I'm a second-generation graduate and a second-generation faculty member. You won't meet many people who've been around here as long as I have," Natalia Belting told me. She had chosen the difficult part of being an historian, and was an assistant professor, a high rank for a woman in a coeducational school. "My father played on the football team when seven of the members were Phi Beta Kappa. That was around 1911 or 1912."

I wanted to talk to Miss Belting to see if someone who had known the University over many years shared the views of newer arrivals. By and large she did. "The old faculty came here and stayed. Now they come, stay for three or five years and leave. And size has made a great difference; when I got my Ph.D. I was secretary to the history department. They needed a Ph.D. in the job because I had to teach when one of the professors was absent, but now they have civil-service secretaries who don't have a professional or even a college background.

"They have access to department heads when other people don't, so that they often exercise academic power they shouldn't. It's a result of size, and the need of professors to delegate authority, but I know of a case concerning one of our most able graduate students who was putting in a lot of time in the quiz section he was teaching. [Quiz sessions are small groups formed from the students who are taking a course in which lectures are being given by a professor. The number in the course is so large that the students are divided into small groups for additional work under a graduate student.] This young man required some written work every week, something most of us should require but we don't have the gumption to assign it, so that five of his students became dissatisfied and wanted to transfer. The secretary told the department head he was making the kids work too hard and that they were coming in and complaining all the time. She caused this graduate student a lot of trouble before we got it straightened out, but she's still there on the same job.

"I know of another case of a boy who had to see his department head for curriculum advice, but couldn't get the secretary to make an appointment for him. She told him there was a rule—which there was—that the head would not see a student without his transcript, and the boy didn't have his, but it is the secretary's job to prepare the transcripts and she hadn't gotten around to it. I'm sure this happens far more than we realize. I feel very sorry for students generally. When there is something that is unfair, most of them are not familiar enough with how the institution works to know what to do, and it's not easy to find someone who does.

"It's a much more difficult school to get through than it was. The student to whom I would give a C today might well have been given an A ten years ago. I don't think it is fair to past or present students.

"You ask why we do it? Don't forget the faculty is on a tough spot. If I give all my class an A, I'll get called on the carpet. It has happened to me once, so the way we grade is not entirely up to us—and yet our relationship is supposed to be exclusively between us and the students."

It had only been bad luck that I hadn't had more time with another woman, the famous Mimsie, Dean of Women. As it was, it was my last day on the campus before I saw her, and she had to squeeze me in without an appointment. She was a good-looking woman of middle years, with charm, a rather large mouth, and a big voice which she used with poised enunciation. I asked her about suicides on the campus, a subject on which there had been considerable vague talk.

"We have them," she admitted. "I don't know how many attempts there are, but I think our statistics probably follow national figures for college students. There are two kinds of suicide attempts, and I never gamble with them. One kind are those that mean it, and the other are those who want attention. We get help to both kinds as fast as we can. I think the young woman who threatens to destroy herself for attention is in as much need of help as the person who intends to do it."

When I mentioned the word *sex,* Mimsie's face took on a droll expression, she exhaled a long sigh, and then moved right in on the subject: "Some of our girls come here without any knowledge. They even lack a basic understanding of a boy's anatomy; and some of them develop almost a sense of power in the petting sequence, by manipulating the boy—emotionally, I mean. Then there is the tragedy of the girl who accepts the boy who says 'I love you.' Of course a lot of this goes back to inadequate training in responsibility for each other. You never know. I do a lot of listening to these kids talk. I'm not sure what they say is fact and what is said in order to appear sophisticated.

"Yes, I know you hear a lot about the housing regulations, but remember a lot of women use them as a crutch to say 'Go home.' Some girls can be overwhelmed, and they need the closing hours as a way of ending the evening. This is especially true of freshmen girls, who are literally pursued. The freshman girl usually can handle her fellow freshman boys, but when it comes to graduate students they are sometimes hard pressed, and your graduate student—when he sees a freshman girl he sees fresh meat. Also, there isn't much to do in this town, after a certain hour, that's legal."

Was the University, or its administrators, truly serious about these regulations, and if it was, why didn't it take obvious enforcement steps like having bed checks?

"There is no bed check because it would be an insult to a young woman. My staff is not a police staff. If I see a violation of the rules, I do something about it, but I don't go out on Friday and Saturday night with my hatchet."

Mimsie had someone waiting to see her, so I said good-bye with the promise that if I got back, I'd buy her a drink.

"I hope you're serious about that," she called through her office door.

Mr. Wilson squirmed in his little office and stared at the disordered papers and books on his desk. He fiddled with his pipe and looked unhappy as I told him that, although his existence isn't too widely known on campus, the people who know of him called him Mr. Clean, or Mr. Fix-it, the man to come to if you wanted something done. All he could say to that was that he certainly tried to be helpful—and it looked like the conversation would get nowhere. Suddenly he interrupted himself to say, "Look, it's true I do a fair amount of freewheeling around here, but the reason I can is nobody knows me. My name never appears in the newspapers." I assured him of anonymity.

He looked happier. "What do you want to know?"

"The first thing I'd like to know is to what extent DDH actually runs the University of Illinois."

"How do you mean?" Wilson said. "He's the president."

"Yes, but does he run it, does he have real power, and how much does he have? It strikes me after going around here for a week or so that DDH is more like the Holy Roman Emperor than a chief executive officer. You know the Holy Roman Emperor was all powerful as long as he just paraded around with his decorations on, but if he ever tried to use his power, his vassals tore him to pieces. Isn't that the way with DDH and his department heads?"

"Somewhat. He has to use a great deal of diplomacy, but he has some power to bargain with. One of his most important tools is the appointing power. He appoints the department chairman and the department heads. He also has the power of *re*appointment."

"But doesn't he have to be very careful about *not* reappointing a department head? Wouldn't he have to worry about the reactions of all the other department heads if he went ahead and just appointed a new man at the end of the old man's term?"

"It is very difficult to appoint a different department head unless there is a division, or dissension in the department, and, on rarer occasions, if the college in which the department is located wants a change of heads."

"Are these the only independent powers he has to contend with? Are there others?"

"Oh, there're others. The colleges have a good deal of independent power, and so does the provost. You should see the provost. Next to the president, he's the most important man in the University. In some ways he has almost as much power, maybe *as* much. It would be very difficult for President Henry if he and the provost didn't agree."

"How much power does the president have through the budget, through controlling the appropriation of money?"

"Not too much. The budgets come up through the departments and the colleges. Of course, the president has a lot of bargaining power when, you might say, there is a deadlock, but mostly the president exercises control through the appointment of committees and steering them through their work."

"You seem to have a committee for everything."

"Don't laugh. It's a system that works, and not all committees are appointed to bury things. We have those kinds of committees, don't mistake me, but we have working committees too, committees that are meant to accomplish something. When you really want to get something done you have to know how to appoint the right committee, and then you get them committed, and whatever it is becomes their idea, their purpose, as much, if not more, than the president's. They use their power and persuasiveness to sell it or get it through whichever way they can."

Switching the subject I asked him about the blatant violations of the housing regulations and the sex problems they betoken. "In asking you about this, I might explain that I am as interested in the administration tactics as I am about the problem itself. How does the administration size up and move on a situation like this?"

"What do you mean exactly?"

"Well, I asked DDH if the University was winking at what was going on and he said certainly not, and he said it in such a way that I think he meant it. I realize it would be difficult for a University president to tell a writer that the rules were being broken, that he knew about it and was doing nothing, but in this case, I had the feeling he really didn't know about it. His reaction was quite emotional."

"I think he feels strongly about it. I wouldn't call him puritanical, but he has very definite standards, and I don't think he does know. I didn't have an idea—I wouldn't have known myself what you meant if a girl had not sat in the chair you're sitting in just a few weeks ago and told me that she spent most of her time in her dorm giving advice about and listening to serious sex problems—you know, like how not to have a baby. A university's pretty much like anyplace else. The person the next rung down isn't going to tell things to the people above him unless there's a point to it or he has to. So as you go up the line, it's natural that people will know less about it. I still don't know very much."

"And DDH knows nothing at all about it?"

"I don't think he does. I'm going to be talking to him about it in a few days."

"Why," I asked him, "was that boy arrested for selling Bibles, particularly after you'd let him sit there for several months? People say the order came from the president's office."

"It didn't. President Henry was not here when it happened.

When he heard about it he was very upset. I can't tell you who ordered it, but it was a mistake. It was a question of somebody's patience wearing thin until he lost his temper. It should never have happened. We lost the case in court."

"Are you saying it should never have happened because you lost the case in court?"

"No, no, not at all. It should *not* have happened. It was very bad for the University, but I think the court decision was way out of line."

"The radical students say that information is given out concerning student's political activities. They say the same of student medical records."

"No records or information of that sort is ever supposed to be given out."

"Yes, but does it happen? Has it happened?"

"Yes, it has happened. We do everything we can to stop these leaks but then it starts again someplace."

"You mean the information is given out without authorization by volunteer junior G-men in the organization, in the bureaucracy?"

"That's exactly what I mean. Volunteer junior G-men describes them. They have no business doing it. We've done everything to stop it, and whenever we hear of another case, we do something about it."

I got up to leave, and Wilson said, "The next time you're back here, we'll have more time, and I'll really tell you something."

The illicit seller of Bibles; John Johnson, the conservative campus politician and uneasy physicist; Richard Traver, the liberal intellectual and writer for the DI—each had achieved a campus renown, overcoming the anonymity that numbers impose. To this list another name, another campus type can be added: Dick Deller, the football player.

A boy may not be able to make a campus reputation as a

football player much longer. The new and seriously purposeful campus cultural styles don't think much of football, although high-caste intellectuals approve of the game because it *is* plebian and disdained by their middle-brow intellectual imitators. Cynics also approve on the grounds it is the only common experience offered members of the modern university academic community.

In the distant past, footballers and athletes weren't even allowed on a campus. Until about the 1820's, collegians who wanted to exercise were told to walk, hunt, or cultivate a garden; athletics were considered undignified, ruffianly, and sinful. The first athletic activity to gain a measure of approval was another German import, gymnastics. Pressure to permit them came from the students, and they were ultimately accepted as a health measure—body building. Extramural athletics in a form we moderns would recognize began on August 3, 1852 at Lake Winnepesaukee. Harvard, in a boat named *Oneida,* beat Yale in a race that constitutes the first intercollegiate athletic contest that anybody knows about.

The next three decades saw development and growth of football and baseball. Like gymnastics, these games also were forced upon the reluctant colleges by their students. In 1873, Andrew White, the president of Cornell, answered an invitation to his school from the University of Michigan to play a game in Cleveland, with his much-quoted message, "I will not permit thirty men to travel four hundred miles merely to agitate a bag of wind."

It has been said that football brought an end to undergraduate violence on the campus by giving the boys another way of working off high spirits. The advent of women on many campuses, relaxation of rules, and the changing nature of the college must have helped to lessen the rough stuff, but if football did help, the price was stiff. In 1905, eighteen players died in football games. President Roosevelt threatened to abolish it.

Dick Deller would hardly recognize the regulated and policed game he was given a scholarship at Illinois to play as the same game the country was up in arms about at the turn of the century, for "There were no codes of rules, and no organizations to enforce any. The purpose of coaches . . . was to win games at any cost and they would themselves sometimes displace players who displeased them—Alonzo Stagg entered the first Chicago-Illinois contest. One early regulation stated that no team might include more than two professionals."

Some colleges gave up football for a time, but most decided to regulate it and began the long tug-of-war to get control of it out of the hands of students and alumni. In doing so, they placed limits on the permissible exploitation of young men such as Dick Deller and gave them an entrée to college that they might not have had.

Dick himself was much shorter than you would expect a football player to be. He was powerfully built; no part of him looked fragile. His broad face was open and without any sign of the aggressiveness that must be his to play such a competitive game so competitively. His neck, hands, and fingers seemed strong and invulnerable.

Although he had gone on to graduate engineering school, he was remembered as the co-captain of the football team the University sent to the Rose Bowl in 1964. It was football that brought him to Champaign: "I was recruited. I picked Illinois because the coaches said if I came here I'd get a good education. I think I have." Without football, he said, he probably would not have been able to go to college, and certainly not one as good as Illinois.

If you aren't a football player and you still want a scholarship to go to college, you might do one of the following to get financial aid:

1. Grow up in Wyoming.
2. Be a descendant of Jaspar Gregory Van Buskirk.
3. Display a breathy desire to fly to the moon.
4. Live in a section of Iowa served by the Chicago, Burlington, and Quincy Railroad.

If you can satisfy number 2 or 4, you are eligible for a Harvard scholarship. Many colleges are encumbered with like eccentric scholarship funds.

Number 1 is a better bet. Colleges, the good private ones, like geographic diversity, but the competition in states without populations is less severe. Also, National Merit Scholarships are apportioned on state quotas, so that a student from a state like Georgia can expect to win a prize even though he does less well in the tests than students in New York or Illinois. The justification for this is that students from states with poor school systems should not be penalized by competing with students from good school systems.

This idea is not applied within a state. Thus in Ohio, students from poor rural and poor Cleveland schools must compete against the products of superior suburban school systems.

Number 3 is good for graduate studies. Many government agencies are passing out fellowship money, but the National Aeronautics and Space Administration, NASA, is particularly beneficent to lunatics.

Many colleges and universities have reservations about scholarships that border on the downright hostile. Restricted gifts like scholarships or professorial chairs have been objected to on the grounds they push universities into activities they have no legitimate business being in by putting money in students' hands to buy education in whatever field happens to be fashionable. Hutchins, writing thirty years before the birth of NASA lunatics, said:

> . . . . If the public becomes interested in the metropolitan newspaper, schools of journalism instantly arise. If it is awed by the development of big business, business schools full of the same reverence appear. If an administration enlarges the activities of the federal government and hence the staff thereof, training for the public service becomes the first duty of the universities. Today public administration, housing . . . are the absorbing subjects of university interest. . . . During the syn-

thetic excitement of the last year [1935, that is] about communism . . . it suddenly became the duty of the colleges and universities to give courses in the eradication of these great evils and in the substitution for them of something called Americanism.

Hutchins also insisted that gifts with strings on them often cost universities more money than they are given. It is a point that has been made time and time again by other administrators as well: "Few restricted gifts have ever been made to a university that paid the expense of receiving them. If men are supported, they are not housed or given the books and equipment they need. If buildings are given, they are not maintained. If they are maintained, they are not manned. From the financial standpoint alone the university may be worse off after the gift than it was before. And from the educational or scientific standpoint it is likely to be unbalanced and confused."

Do students who need financial help get it? Or, are students who can pay their own way getting help they don't really need? A robust, if conflicting, research literature has grown up around such points. The best that can be said with certainty is that the administration of scholarship programs might be improved.

There is, for example, evidence to show that about 20 percent of the students receiving aid are from relatively high-income families. There is also evidence to show that many students, if denied aid, would be able and willing to continue their studies. At the other end of the stick, the figures show that apparently many students who have the mental machinery but not the money to go through college are not getting help.

Underneath the question of scholarship apportionment is a larger one: There exists no thought-out national policy on the purposes of aid to students or institutions. Thus, people will disagree about the public's obligation to help pay for a given student's education and ignore our general social need for educated people.

If it were football that brought Dick Deller a scholarship and an education, it was also football that brought him something else—satisfaction on the campus.

Like many busy students in engineering, but unlike John Johnson or Richard Traver, Dick wasn't an active campus figure during his undergraduate days. "I was on a committee on student values but it sort of fell through. We had two or three meetings but only about half the people could get there. The committee was set up to ask 'What is the problem with student values?' 'Is there one?'"

The engineering school gave Dick no breaks on courses or marks, so that he had to budget his energy and time carefully. The most he got in the way of an academic concession was a short postponement on a paper or an exam because of the football schedule, but even this he could never be sure of. It depended on the teacher.

"During the football season you've got to get more sleep than if you weren't playing," Dick said. "As the season goes on, the practices get lighter, which helps. I tried not to get too far behind at the beginning, and I decided to take an extra semester [so as not to carry too big a load] and to balance two tough courses with an easy one [quite common in the engineering school]."

Dick lived in a trailer near the University with his wife, Karen, a tall, somewhat intense, ex-sorority girl. However unpromising living in a trailer may sound, it is in fact quite comfortable— once inside their living room, you would forget you were not in a duly constructed house. Being the star football player's girl, while fun, Karen said, had its anxious times too. "Before Saturday dances I was worried I wouldn't have a date because the man on the radio kept saying 'on the bottom of the pile is Dick Deller.' We had a religious problem too. [Dick is a Catholic.] And once we separated from 2:00 A.M. till about ten o'clock in the next morning."

Dick sat next to Karen on their living-room couch, ruffled her hair a little, and expressed content: "But here we are, and it worked out fine."

Karen worked for the phone company after having majored in personnel management: "Most of the courses I took were in economics. I started out in liberal arts, but actually when I came down here I didn't know what I was going to do. Talk about a confused freshman! I took about a year and a half of it, and then got into commerce, but I had to work two semesters to talk my adviser into letting me out of liberal arts. We had a big fight. Now I'm at the phone company as a group chief, the first level of management. I don't think my training has helped me specifically on the job, but it meant something that I went to college. I'm grateful that I did."

Generally the young Dellers were grateful; grateful to the University, and grateful to the Greek system that had brought them together. Karen added that the sorority did something else:

"When I was a freshman I was scared of everything. I'm still not an extrovert but I really think if I had ever been put in a big dormitory like Allen, I wouldn't have fought it out but would have packed up and gone home. It was so much better at Tri-Delt House with all the smiling faces. It made me feel like somebody cared."

Dick concurred: "In a dorm you may be all alone. I didn't know a soul here when I arrived except a few coaches. It was scary."

Big institutions can scare anybody, even big football players. Karen and Dick found ways of making the University a homey place for themselves. For others, Illinois, in common with all universities, has a special orientation program to reduce freshman cultural shock. Before school starts, freshmen are brought to campus for counseling. They are also given a list of books—respectable ones by people like social critics Jacques Barzun and C. P. Snow, semanticist S. I. Hayakawa, and diplomatic historian George F. Kennan. The students must pick two from the

191

list and read them; the student who does will be warned that the University is no romper room.

When the freshmen get to the University, they start their new collegiate life with New Student Week; they are loaded down with printed matter including *Illini Guidelines* (93 pages), a book called *Undergraduate Courses* (233 pages), and another book called *Undergraduate Study* (384 pages).

But during the week the freshmen are not left to puzzle things out for themselves with only the printed matter to aid them. New Student Week has the freshmen going to student mixers, meeting with the deans, having conferences with their colleges (the University is divided into twenty colleges and schools of which the biggest is the College of Liberal Arts and Sciences). By means of a special closed-circuit television program, the provost speaks to small groups of students who, with faculty members, watch from TV sets throughout the campus, then discuss what was said with "student leaders." There are also a registration dance, special services at all campus churches, open houses at the YM and YW, a convocation with a famous guest speaker (preferably an alumnus), musical selections by the choir and band, and a welcoming address by President Henry, followed by a reception in the Assembly Hall Concourse.

The freshmen are now supposed to be ready to begin work, and judging by the record, two-thirds of them are, although the rest have merely taken the first step out the door.

Less attention is paid to him, but the young teacher may find his first encounter with the school as painful as the students'. But there is no orientation week to slide him into accommodation with institutional reality:

A young man who likes to teach and may develop into a research man is asked to a college or a university by a department head who says, "Now, we older men here have never had much time to do research. We are going to create a special position for you, so that you can help us build up the department. You will have some advanced courses from the start, and you will have time for a seminar and a little research."

When he gets there he is met with this: "We're sorry. The enrollments are a bit bigger than expected, so you will have to teach more sections of the introductory course. Besides, the dean didn't quite understand the situation. But next year, you can get along with the original plan. Hope you don't mind. We have all had to take our turn at these chores." By about the third year, when he presses things a bit, he is told, "Well, who the hell do you think you are to think you should have privileges the rest of us never got?" There are many varieties of this sophomoric initiation. If the young man organizes his courses in his own way . . . the dean may call him in to say, "Now isn't it fine that you want to outline a course in your own way. But are you sure you have it well organized? The students complain that they never know what tomorrow's assignment is. Maybe you should use a textbook until you have had a little more experience." . . . There is no need to tell you these are devices used on eager newcomers in industry, the army, and reform schools.

. . . It is amazing how quickly academic people can lose their identity with the world of excellence and join with the home guards to prevent change.

13

It's Safer in the Dorms

"I don't think it'll break down. It's got the Chicago habit. It's always made Chicago. It breaks down when it goes someplace else."

Tammy, a spirited girl with pigtails, Priscilla, and I were in Alex's car, whose odometer registered in the vicinity of 98,000 miles. It, and we in it, were driving north toward Chicago at its cautious top speed through the cornfields that the University's sophisticates are so self-conscious about. Our take-off from Champaign earlier had been highly studential. First, we had to move Tammy's roommate from their "approved housing" to Alex's garret apartment because this "approved housing" closes during the Christmas vacation—probably because the "approved person" (that is, chaperone, warden, or matron as you may view the University's regulations) wanted to go home for Christmas.

I had met Alex, who was a very contrasty person, earlier in the week. In a black leather jacket and a white crash helmet, he had looked like one of those motorized thugs they make decrying movies about. He had a handsome but jagged face which inspired misgivings until he opened his well-spoken mouth and told you he was getting his master's degree in industrial relations.

Alex was going home for the holidays, so Tammy's roommate

was to take possession of his tiny apartment, with his excellent photographs on the wall. Alex had to stop and get a key made, and after he'd gotten the key made he had to stop again and give the key to someone, after which Tammy remembered she had forgotten to bring her Christmas present "for my man," which in turn reminded Alex that he had left his bike outside and that he had better put it away lest it be stolen, and finally we couldn't go anywhere without gas in the tank, would everybody please contribute?

"Tam," Alex said as we went along, "did I tell you I finished that paper on Marx?"

"Great. God, I want to get out of this curriculum [biology] and write papers in things I'm interested in. Hey, guess what? Guess what Terry got? She got a $200 scholarship! Came in the mail this morning."

There was talk of scholarships for a few miles, easy-to-get scholarships, good scholarships, and how to get them. Then Alex boasted he had a new recording and Tammy accused him of having "a rich woman, a woman with money."

"I do."

"How'd you get her?"

"Ran her over with my bicycle one day."

More miles and more chitchat, and then Tammy asked me, "What do you think of the University?"

"I don't think it's a machine."

"Well, what do you think it *is?*"

"It may possibly be the world's largest amoeba. It may not know what it's doing; it certainly has a primitive nervous system, and communication between the parts is pretty uncertain, but it's not a machine. It's alive; it senses things and people." I told them a little bit of Melinda's story, and commented, "It may not have handled Melinda well, but it sensed she was in some kind of trouble; it may have bumbled and fumbled, but it did get her some kind of help. The way it did it is amoeba-like—no eyes, no ears, just by sensing with its pseudopods."

195

"Great! You going to put that in your book?"

"I think so."

"They'll die—but it's not like an amoeba."

"Oh? What's it like?"

"It's like euglena. It's much more like euglena. [Euglena is another, slightly more complicated one-celled lady.] Euglena's got a flagellum, and euglena's more complicated than amoeba—and the University's complicated. Euglena reproduces by binary fission like the University. [She has in mind the huge new campus, virtually another university, that opened in Chicago.] Definitely euglena."

We went some more miles down the road when Tammy said, "I'm hungry."

"I'm starved," said Alex.

"I'm famished," said Priscilla.

Not far from Kankakee a smorgasbord all-you-can-eat place was sighted, but when we went inside it looked expensive. There was a consultation about money, and I offered to treat.

"Good," Tammy said and began the first of her three trips to the steam table. In this she was accompanied by Priscilla, who told me, "I guess it's the result of being freed from dorm food." Alex ate about what a hungry man of his age and station usually eats, or half of what the girls put down.

Back on the road I asked Tammy how many girls does she share her room with. "Four, but we've had five."

"Five! Since when have you had five there, Tam?" Alex asked.

"Have you forgotten Sally already?"

"Oh, Sally."

"Who's Sally?"

"That's a long story," he said.

"Tell him about Sally, Alex."

"Meg Rowe—the girl who quit to work among the Kentucky miners—called up one morning and said she was down at a diner in Champaign. She had returned on a flying visit. She said I should come right over, that she couldn't tell me any more about it. I'm pretty terrible in the morning—I don't feel good and I don't act good—but Meg is Meg, so I got dressed and went over and there she was, her same fat self with this girl, a stray she had brought up from Kentucky. The girl had told Meg this story about how they were trying to put her in an insane asylum. We found out later it was a lie, but Meg was always gullible. She said they couldn't put her away after she reached her eighteenth birthday and she asked us to keep her here in Illinois until she was eighteen, which was very soon."

"We thought she really was a victim of injustice," Tammy interrupted. "You couldn't, you absolutely couldn't tell from meeting her. You had to get to know her. She was so shy, and she seemed to be afraid. I mean she just looked and acted like a victim of injustice."

Alex went on to tell how the group got Sally an apartment and found her a job as a waitress and then discovered she was writing little notes on the paper napkins, inviting her male customers to visit her. So they got her out of the restaurant and brought her to Tammy's place to keep an eye on her.

"You really had to baby-sit with her, really baby-sit," Tammy said. "We couldn't leave her alone. If we left her alone she would be gone with a man, drinking, everything. We had to have somebody there to watch her all the time. And she'd borrow money or drink your beer. She had no idea of how little money students have. She'd borrow it and say she was going to pay it back, and at first I believed her."

Finally, they gave up on her and a sheriff came up from Kentucky to take her back home. When this happened, the students felt guilty that they had betrayed Sally and wished they had not had a hand in her being taken.

They went to the local jail, where she was waiting for the Kentucky people to take her back, and they were not permitted to visit her. They kicked up a fuss but then dropped Sally's possessions and walked out, perplexed at themselves, feeling guilty, and not knowing what else they might have done.

The affair puzzled them. They had treated the girl just as Mimsie would have. They had tried to get her to obey all the conventional rules they say they do not believe in. The girl's wanton use of her personal freedom had been dangerous and destructive to them. When they talked about it, they were uncertain about freedom from the University, freedom so liberating, so frightening, so uncertain.

"If we'd been living in the dorms it could never have happened," Tammy said. "Nothing like that ever happens in the dorms. It's safe there. Nobody ever gets knocked up and everybody passes."

Notes

Page 10 Herbert Muller, *The Uses of the Past: Profiles of Former Societies* (New York: Oxford University Press [Galaxy], 1957), p. 51.

13–14 Allan Nevins, *Illinois* (New York: Oxford University Press, 1917), pp. 34–35.

25 David Riesman and Christopher Jencks, "The Viability of the American College," in *The American College*, ed. Nevitt Sanford (New York: John Wiley and Sons, Inc., 1962), p. 126.

26 *Ibid.*, pp. 101, 113.

27 *Ibid.*, p. 76.

28 *The Yale Report of 1828*, as cited in *American Higher Education: A Documentary History* (hereafter cited as Hofstadter-Smith), edited by Richard Hofstadter and Wilson Smith (Chicago: University of Chicago Press, 1961), I, pp. 278, 282.

29 Riesman, *op. cit.*, p. 83.

30 *Ibid.*, pp. 84–85.

31 Francis Wayland, *Thoughts on the Present Collegiate System in the United States* (Boston, 1842), as cited in Hofstadter-Smith, I, pp. 358–359.

32 Henry P. Tappan, *University Education* (New York, 1851), as cited in Hofstadter-Smith, II, pp. 490, 492, 493.

33 Bernard Berelson, *Graduate Education in the United States* (New York: McGraw-Hill Book Company, Inc., 1962), p. 56.

34–35 Daniel Cort Gilman, *Johns Hopkins University Celebration of the Twenty-fifth Anniversary of the Founding* (Baltimore, 1902), as cited in Hofstadter-Smith, II, pp. 646, 648.

35 Henry Seidel Canby, *Alma Mater: The Gothic Age of the American College* (New York: Farrar and Rinehart, Inc., 1936), pp. 60–61.

35, 192 Seymour E. Harris, *Higher Education: Resources and Finance* (New York: McGraw-Hill Book Company, Inc., 1962).

41 R. T. Crane, *The Demoralization of College Life* (Chicago: H. O. Shepard and Co., 1911), p. 18.

43 G. Stanley Hall, *Life and Confessions of a Psychologist* (New York: Appleton-Century-Crofts, Inc., 1923), pp. 295–96.

44–45 Wade Thompson, "Custodians of the Language Convene," *The Nation*, CC, No. 6, pp. 145–146.

57–58 J. H. Fairchild, *Oberlin, Its Origin, Progress, and Results. An Address.*

... *1860* (Oberlin, 1871), as cited in Hofstadter-Smith, I, pp. 428–429.

59   James Weschler, *Revolt on Campus* (New York: Covici-Friede, 1935), pp. 101, 115–116.

62–63   David Riesman, *Constraint and Variety in American Education* (Lincoln, Nebr.: University of Nebraska Press, 1956), pp. 29–31.

64–65   Logan Wilson, *The Academic Man* (New York: Oxford University Press, 1942), pp. 195, 197.

65   Theodore Caplow and Reece J. McGee, *The Academic Marketplace* (New York: Basic Books, Inc., 1958), p. 83.

69   Alexander Meiklejohn, "What the Liberal College Is," in *The Liberal College* (Boston, 1920), as cited in Hofstadter-Smith, II, pp. 897–898.

69   John Witherspoon, *Address to the Inhabitants of Jamaica, and Other West Indian Islands in Behalf of the College of New Jersey* (Philadelphia, 1772), as cited in Hofstadter-Smith, I, p. 440.

70   George Wilson Pierson, *Yale College, 1871–1921* (New Haven: Yale University Press, 1952), pp. 32, 34–35.

71   Everett Lee Hunt, *The Revolt of the College Intellectual* (New York: Human Relations Aids, 1963), p. 78.

72   *Ibid.*, pp. 93, 72.

73   *Ibid.*, p. 99.

87   Frederick Rudolph, *Mark Hopkins and the Log* (New Haven: Yale University Press, 1956), p. 16.

88–89   Robert M. Hutchins, *The Higher Learning in America* (New Haven: Yale University Press, 1936), pp. 1–2.

90   James McCosh, *The New Departure in College Education, Being a Reply to President Eliot's Defense of It in New York* (New York, 1885), as cited in Hofstadter-Smith, II, pp. 716, 720.

90   "The Trustees of Dartmouth College v. Woodward," in *Reports of Cases Signed and Decided in the Supreme Court of the United States,* IV (Newark, N.J., 1882), as cited in Hofstadter-Smith, I, pp. 212–213.

91   Thomas Jefferson to George Ticknor, Monticello, July 16, 1823, Jefferson MSS, Vol. CCXXIV., Library of Congress.

92   A 1754 newspaper advertisement. From *The New York Gazette* or *Weekly Post-Boy,* No. 592 (June 3, 1754).

92–93   L. J. Halser, ed., *The Works of Philip Lindsley* (Philadelphia, 1866), as cited in Hofstadter-Smith, I, pp. 233, 331, 333.

94   ["Over seven hundred colleges . . ."] Frederick Rudolph, *The American College and University: A History* (New York: Alfred A. Knopf, Inc., 1962), p. 218.

95   Francis Wayland, *Thoughts on the Present Collegiate System in the United States* (Boston, 1842), as cited in Hofstadter-Smith, I, pp. 357–358.

97   Charles William Eliot. Cited in Samuel Eliot Morison, *Three Centuries of Harvard* (Cambridge, Mass.: Harvard University Press, 1936), pp. 329–330.

99–100   [Dropouts.] John Summerskill, "Dropouts from College," in Nevitt Sanford, *op. cit.,* pp. 631, 637.

101   Robert M. Hutchins, *op. cit.,* pp. 11–12.

113–114   [Wittgenstein.] Norman Malcolm, *Ludwig Wittgenstein, a Memoir* (New York: Oxford University Press, 1958), pp. 26–27.

117   [pictures of a professor . . .] Robert H. Knapp, "Changing Functions of the College Professor," in Nevitt Sanford, *op. cit.,* p. 289.

118   President Sturtevant, Letter of J. M. Sturtevant to Theron Baldwin, cited in Charles Henry Rammelkamp, *Illinois College: A Centennial History, 1829–1929* (New Haven: Yale University Press, 1928), p. 141.

118   Charles Henry Rammelkamp, *ibid.,* p. 261.

122   Philip E. Jacob, *Changing Values in College: An Exploratory Study of the Impact of College Teaching* (New York: Harper & Row, 1957), pp. 199–200.

122   Rose K. Goldsen and others, *What College Students Think* (Princeton, N.J.: D. Van Nostrand Co.), p. 16.

129   Thorstein Veblen, *The Higher Learning in America: A Memorandum on the Conduct of Universities by Businessmen* (New York: The Viking Press, 1918), pp. 103–105, 166.

136   Thomas Jefferson Wertenbaker, *Princeton, 1746–1896* (Princeton, N.J.: Princeton University Press, 1946), p. 161.

137   Frederick A. P. Barnard, *Letters on College Government* (New York, 1896), as cited in Hofstadter-Smith, I, pp. 511–513.

145–146   [the way teaching was done at Yale in the 1820's . . .] Julian M. Sturtevant, *An Autobiography* (New York, 1896), pp. 84–85, 90–91.

146–147   Wigglesworth. Cited in Samuel Eliot Morison, *op. cit.,* p. 67.

147   George Ticknor to Thomas Jefferson, Boston, June 16, 1823, Jefferson MSS. Vol. CCXXIV, Library of Congress.

148–149   [Beard's resignation.] Beard to Butler, Oct. 8, 1917, Minutes of the Trustees of Columbia University, XXXVIII (1917–1918).

150–151   Abbott Lawrence Lowell, "Academic Freedom," in *At War With Academic Traditions in America* (Cambridge, Mass.: Harvard University Press, 1934), pp. 269, 272.

152–153   [the idea of the ideal teacher . . .] Joseph Adelson, "The Teacher as Model," in Nevitt Sanford, *op. cit.,* pp. 407–412.

153   Irwin Silber, "Songs from Berkeley," *Sing Out!* XV, No. 2 (1965), p. 18.

153–154   Thorstein Veblen, *op. cit.,* pp. 220–222.

160   ["Not every president . . .] George P. Schmidt, *The Old-Time College President* (New York: Columbia University Press, 1930), p. 63.

161   *Ibid.,* p. 105.

187   ["There were no codes of rules . . ."] Allan Nevins, *op. cit.,* p. 202.

188–189   Robert M. Hutchins, *op. cit.,* pp. 5–6.